THE LIFE IN MY YEARS

VIRGINIA McKENNA

The Life in My Years

OBERON BOOKS
LONDON

First published in 2009 by Oberon Books Ltd

521 Caledonian Road, London N7 9RH

tel 020 7607 3637 / fax 020 7607 3629

info@oberonbooks.com / www.oberonbooks.com

A catalogue record for this book is available from the British Library.

ISBN: 978-1-84002-898-0

Printed by CPI Antony Rowe Ltd, Chippenham

Contents

Foreword by Joanna Lumley

I MUST HAVE BEEN ABOUT fourteen years old when I first knew the name of Virginia McKenna. She seemed to be almost unbearably beautiful, a famous film star, and as remote as the moon from our childhood world of boarding schools and mucking about on the farms in the holidays. My kind of acting was being in the school play and there seemed to be no possible link between being Aaron in Christopher Fry's *The Firstborn* (I often played boys and men, and my chin was always covered with glued-on beards, my thighs often slapped with a deep merry laugh) and actually turning into another real person, with a camera inches from your face. She did it though, and in hauntingly memorable films too. I think she was the first actress I longed to be like, but apart from a rumour that her mother had bought a house I had once stayed in ('No! So she might have walked about looking at the rooms! and seen where we slept! Gosh!!') there was no chance that our paths would ever cross. It was more likely that pigs might fly.

Why did I admire her so? Because she always inhabited the character she played completely, and never sounded ill-at-ease with her lines (it's quite an art to make the words sound as though you are speaking them for the first time): and because she was serene, and because the people she had been chosen to portray were often heroines, and because she moved well and was... heck, she was a star.

YEARS LATER, because the world is small and life is short, my career galloped me along to the position where I could be asked to appear in charity shows; and it was at one such, at the Garrick Theatre, when she and her daughter Louise were singing a duet (singing? how did I miss that she could sing like a bird as well?) that I approached her. I said that I was very sad to hear of the dreadful end of Pole Pole, the little elephant she and her husband Bill Travers had been filming with, and if there was anything I could do, I would.

She was slighter than I imagined, very small-boned and fragile to look at and exceptionally beautiful. (Louise was exquisite too: in the prompt corner of the theatre I heard the late Christopher Reeve say: 'Who *is* that girl? I have to know her.') Virginia turned to me and said 'We have just started something; I'll let you know'. And she did, and it was Zoo Check.

This was long before it was usual for famous people to start charities or even really to support them; and it seemed so right and daring that these two giants of the screen should use the springboard of the film *Born Free* to bring the country's attention to how dreadful zoos are. It wasn't easy; the customary arguments were raised ('I suppose you care more for animals than children'... 'they are safe in zoos and must be happy because they are eating'... 'but not everyone can go to Africa to see an elephant'), but with iron determination and impeccable manners the Travers husband and wife team (as they were now called) began to turn the tide of public opinion.

Above all, they made us think of what freedom really is, and how it is the most longed-for right in existence. When someone is punished we take away their freedom because, short of killing them, it's the worst thing we can do to them. Watch any creature in confinement and it will take the chance to escape if it can. Bill once told me never to forget that every animal is unique and has its own character: each sad lion in a circus ring, each shabby bear in a fake rocky cage has just as many idiosyncrasies as our own beloved household pets: ('Smokey won't eat unless I put the dish beside the cooker; Rover always remembers Aunt Mary and growls when she gets out of the car').

BILL AND VIRGINIA: Virginia and Bill. It's not surprising she starts and ends the book with Bill; they were as close as Baucis and Philemon whom the gods made into twin trees when they died. Her achievement as an actress is one thing, her continuation of the work she and Bill started is quite another. The pages are full of yearning and remembrances, not bitter, but infinitely poignant to those of us who knew them both (well, we all did, you and I; they were our people on the screen, our stars and heroes).

She has made a sort of scrapbook of her life in this book, flitting forwards and backwards, rich in details of filming, of family, friends and animals, and of her great passion for nature. I like to think it is as though we are sitting in a grand hotel room, or, far better, a shady garden… Yes! as though I am interviewing her, and meeting her for the very first time! Sometimes we stop for a cup of tea, sometimes I ask her to elaborate on something, sometimes we sit in quietness or hear her speak her poetry. (Oh, didn't I say that? She is a poet as well as everything else.) What we have here is Virginia McKenna as she sees herself; her life, full of passion and grace and fun and wisdom and friendship, is the main feature tonight, so settle back as the lights dim and watch her as she appears as herself in her greatest role of all.

Prologue

W HEN I WAS THINKING about writing a memoir in 2006,
I turned to an old friend, Adrian House, whom I first met
in the 1960s. Adrian, who was then an editor at Collins
and is now a much admired author, looked at the first few pages and
encouraged me to continue. He provided excellent guidelines. I'm
not sure I have followed them successfully! Memory has its own way
of leading you on, but what is certain is that it took me to the end of
2008! It is only in that sense that it is chronological. The book itself
is a random glimpse into the experiences I have had, the people and
animals I have known. Yet everything is connected in some way.

It has been a strange book to undertake, quite different from
those I have written in the past: *Into the Blue*; *Some of my Friends Have
Tails*; *On Playing with Lions* (with my husband, Bill); *Beyond the Bars*,
to which I was a contributor. In this book I have been on a personal
journey. Sometimes surprising myself by what I remember, sometimes ashamed at what I have forgotten; always interested in what is
to come. Perhaps at the heart of it is my regret that nowhere can I
read about my parents and grandparents. My daughter, Louise, often
wants to talk about family stories and I can only tell her the ones
from my personal experience.

Much as I would have liked to, it has been impossible to mention
every friend by name, and equally to express my appreciation to all
the wonderful individuals who work alongside us at the Born Free
Foundation. I hope they will forgive me!

This year, 2009, is the twenty-fifth anniversary of the Foundation,
which Bill, Will, our eldest son and I started (as Zoo Check) in 1984.
One of our events is a week at the Royal Geographical Society. Funded,
as always, by our loyal sponsor Land Rover, we will be looking back at
the work we have done over the last quarter of a century, the joys and
the heartaches. But the major occasion, an anniversary concert, will
be held in a building which, in a way, brings my life full circle.

The Royal Albert Hall. Home of The Central School of Speech
and Drama during my student days in the 1940s. Scene of fencing

lessons, mime, diction, movement, rehearsal and performance. The place where I took my first steps into adult life and anticipated the excitement at what might lie ahead.

If I am honest, when I started writing this book I didn't even know if I would finish it. I just put things down as they came into my head or my heart. Snapshots of this wonderful, joyous, sometimes lonely, sometimes deeply sad, exciting, challenging experience that has been my life. Up to now.

Acknowledgements

MY SON Will gave me a fridge magnet which reads: '*It is not the years in your life that count but the life in your years*'. I thank both him and Abraham Lincoln for providing me with the title for this book.

There are many people who have helped me with individual expertise, patience and encouragement. At the top of this list must be Elizabeth Zetter who, amazingly, managed to decipher my increasingly illegible handwriting and blobs from different coloured marker pens, as I altered and inserted and eliminated.

I realised early on how fortunate I have been to have Oberon as my publisher. I am deeply grateful to James Hogan for his advice, to Production Manager Stephen Watson, to Daisy Bowie-Sell in the Editorial Department, to Design Consultant Jon Morgan, and to all the members of the supportive Oberon team.

Thanks to all the photographers, some of whom have generously given their photographs for this book.

At Born Free I have had very special help from Sarah Stead in my office, and from Claire Stanford, Angelique Davies and Tricia Holford who have promptly and cheerfully responded to my queries about photos and facts.

I had always hoped that Joanna Lumley would write the foreword but it was with some hesitation that I phoned her and asked her. In her typically generous and open-hearted way she immediately said she would. 'Thank you' seems inadequate.

To my agents, Diana Tyler and David Riding at MBA I am truly grateful for, first of all, wanting to represent me and, second, for looking after me so well.

And lastly - my family. They have been a tower of strength as always. I thank them for being the real motivation and inspiration behind the whole challenge.

Dedicated to my family, to my friends and to animals everywhere.

You Can See Forever

2006

MY HUSBAND BILL TRAVERS, actor, film-maker and animal campaigner, died twelve years ago. He is buried in our village churchyard – next to my mother's grave. When I die I shall share his space. I like that idea. I like to talk about 'when I go' – not in a macabre or soppy way but realistically. I like to plan which of my children and grandchildren will inherit the pictures, the pieces of furniture and jewellery that have meant a lot to me and to Bill. Things that have been touched by loving hands. Some of the furniture is very old and belonged to my grandmother (my mother's mother), whom I adored. There won't be a lot of money to leave them as now I rarely work as an actress. Not that Bill and I were rich – if we did earn something we spent it on our garden, our children's education, his documentary films, our home and our holiday house in Sardinia. That house may soon be sold. And that's all right too.

Top left: Enjoying a tea-break with our lovely builders!

Above: Our house in Surrey when we bought it.

Left: Bill planting the cherry tree in the garden.

Bottom left: Rehearsing for my parachute jump in Carve Her Name with Pride.

Below: Our wedding.

Bottom right: Honeymooning in Paris.

Virginia McKenna

Everything has its time. We had joyous holidays there for thirty years, but not only have the dynamics of our family changed now but so has the part of Sardinia where we built the house. Time to let go.

My feelings for our Surrey home are different. This year I will have lived in it for 49 years. We planted most of the trees in the garden and my roots are dug deep too. The main thing is the view. You can see forever. The North Downs dimly edge the far sky as we look down from our 650-foot hill. We'd had our name down on estate agents' lists for two years - some houses we saw were horrendous, some too perfect, but the little bathroom-less cottage - well, we thought it was perfect for us. Because of its setting, the view, the peace, the woodland that bordered the sloping field. We came down one weekend and planted a cherry tree.

For two months we lived in a caravan on the edge of the woods while the lovely Irish builders put in a bathroom and changed a few things inside. It was heaven. We were both working hard. Bill had just done *A Cook for Mr General* in New York for Kraft Television Theatre TV and I was at Pinewood Studios filming *Carve Her Name with Pride*, the story of Violette Szabo, the extraordinary, courageous woman who worked in Special Operations Executive (SOE) in occupied France in the Second World War. We had yet to marry as we had both been married before and my divorce had still to come through. But we lived together - controversial in those days. We couldn't bear to be apart. Halfway through filming I was suddenly free. It had taken three years. I shall always remember that moment. I was in Abingdon, being taught how to jump off a high platform, wearing a parachute harness and a hat that looked like a doughnut, and to land correctly. As I waited to leap off I saw Bill, who had come there with me, suddenly get up and walk into a side room. Just as I was to 'take off' he came back, hugely smiling, and gave me a thumbs-up sign. My heart was as light as a feather as I drifted to the ground. I was given a long weekend off to get married and go to Paris for our honeymoon. Never had I been so happy.

Childhood

WHEN YOU WRITE THINGS down all sorts of pictures and memories flash inside your head, beautiful, radiant. But not all of them are prettily coloured; some re-open wounds that one thought had healed. Others remind you that some questions will never be answered.

So it is pointless regretting you never knew your parents better, never asked questions which only they could have answered. Questions about their childhood and struggles, whether they had found fulfilment, happiness, if only in a transitory way.

When I was at boarding school in Sussex after the war I was quite often invited to stay the weekend with a girl I'd made friends with. Her family lived in the country, had a farm, and she had two brothers and a sister. A real family. I loved it. I watched the sweet affection between the parents with wonder as I had never really seen love expressed in that way. It was heart-stopping.

My own childhood, as an only child, had been very different; my parents parted when I was four. I lived with my father and nanny Mary Stringer in London until I was seven when we moved to the country, near Horsham. My father was a handsome, charming, clever man, a great reader. He suffered from poor health and had to leave his job as one of Christie's chief auctioneers before the war. He was a brilliant auctioneer and, with his debonair good looks, a familiar figure in the well-known salerooms of which he was also a partner. In 1929 he conducted the auction of the famous Portland Vase, reaching a price of £29,000 in only 60 seconds - though the reserve price was never attained! Although he had retired he returned to Christie's during the war to conduct some sales in aid of the Red Cross.

His expertise was in jewellery - and it made me think of the jewellery my mother had to sell when my father lost his money. It must have been very special. He also loved the theatre and I remember being taken by him to see a play starring Fay Compton, his cousin on his mother's side (the Mackenzies). Although he never became an actor there must have been a strong 'theatrical' feeling running through the McKenna/Mackenzie family. I have an amazing old family photo album filled with sepia memories of my father and his brothers when they were very small – dressed up in the most fantastic costumes. Napoleon, a caveman, Robin Hood, a monk – on it went! What fun it would have been to ask him about all this.

It must have been very hard for him to bring up a little girl on his own, and I don't recall many times when we played or talked together. My 'rock' till I was seven was my nanny and, following our move, Phyllis – who had been my father's housekeeper. I kept in touch with them both until they died. I really loved them. So, in a way, I suppose my father had no option but to send me to weekly boarding school in 1938, when I was seven. I was unhappy there, I can't deny it, and being rather reserved I was easily intimidated by some of the other girls. I particularly dreaded bedtime. One girl, the ringleader, would say goodnight to all the others, by name, but not me. It was a nightmare and I wished with all my heart I was a million miles away!

But for some reason everything changed the next term. This same girl met me walking by the little stream at the bottom of the garden on the first day back at school, and asked me if I would like to be friends! Anyway, you learn to deal with these things if you're on your own, and by the time the war came and my father, in 1940, decided to send me to South Africa for as long as the war lasted, I had settled down and was reasonably content. The school itself was lovely – small, unpretentious, run by two very intelligent and kind headmistresses – and (although I didn't know it at that time) the place where the seed was planted that would lead me into acting.

⌣

THE EXPERIENCE of going to South Africa was surreal. My mother was to take me. She had given up her flourishing career as a pianist and cabaret artist to take this young girl into the unknown. As Anne de Nys, she was part of a trio – 'That Certain Trio', with the singer Patrick Waddington and John Ridley as second pianist – and played before the war at the Savoy, the Berkeley and other prestigious London venues. It was only as an adult that I began to appreciate the enormity of what she had given up and taken on. A journey to a far-off land, an uncertain future, with a nine-year-old daughter she had only seen during visiting weekends. Neither of us knew each other at all. It was daunting. We were in a convoy of five ships leaving Liverpool

Above left: My father in 1898, as Napoleon - with friend!

Above right: With my father and nanny Mary Stringer in London.

Below: My father's housekeeper Phyllis Jones.

Right: My mother's piano trio 'That Certain Trio', with John Ridley and Patrick Waddington.

"THAT CERTAIN TRIO"

JOHN RIDLEY   ANNE DE NYS   PATRICK WADDINGTON

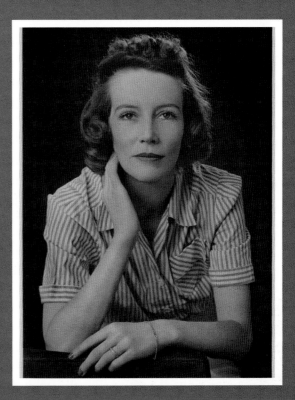

Above: Photomontage of my mother and me on the Etretat cliffs.

Right: My mother in South Africa.

Below: On the ship to South Africa.

Bottom left: With Simon the cocker spaniel.

Bottom right: With our housekeeper Ethel Maquenukana and Blitzy.

for Cape Town – on the last, which was then held back by an air raid warning. The other four ships were all torpedoed. We saw the debris floating on the water. I can still see it.

⌣

THE TABLE I am touching is made of old ships' timbers. The family dining table, the scene of laughter, argument, discussion, joking, sadness, silence. The moments that most families experience. I think I am quite old-fashioned – family mealtimes have always been very important to me. Now, obviously, they are more infrequent but when everyone is gathered round and small grandchildren's voices and chatter fill the air, I'm in heaven. The planning and cooking of the meal, the chopping and stirring and peeling, the classical music on the radio spurring me on to wilder concoctions – these are always happy moments.

I've been thinking of my mother in her old age, bent and sad, and her last mealtimes at this table. She was a very attractive, vivacious person with a wide circle of friends where she lived in the South of France. Her father was French and we always teased my mother that she was more French than the French. She adored France and eventually gave up her flat in London and went permanently to live in Antibes. She always came to us for Christmas, as did her eldest brother Peter, and usually in the summer as well. Tragically, her happy life was changed in an instant by an accident – a car knocked her down as it was backing out of a space in a car park, her hip broke and the last nightmare eight years of her life began. It wasn't just a question of operations going wrong, endless painkillers, endless searches for other surgeons to correct the mistakes. That was bad enough. It was the bitterness that changed her personality – the fact that she could never forgive the driver of the car, never come to terms with the new kind of life she had to face. Fiercely independent, she found my decision to sell her car emotionally unacceptable and when, finally, it was impossible to make sure she was properly cared for so far away, I had to bring her to England and sell her flat, it was traumatic for her. Eventually I found a lovely residential home for her nearby where she could be well nursed and looked after and where the family and her friends could visit her. So this all came back to me. It wasn't always like that of course – she loved Bill and he would tease her and laugh

Virginia McKenna

with her and make her feel special. 'Straighten up Annie', he'd say, and she would jolt upright – just for a few minutes and then her back would bend again. Osteoporosis was to be her destiny.

My mother was a fine musician – played everything by ear, had perfect pitch and, happily, her talent passed on to our daughter Louise – and to her daughters. But when the music left my mother's soul it left her hands as well. She no longer wanted to play or, finally, even to listen to music. Perhaps it brought back memories that overwhelmed her with sadness.

I wish I had been able to share more of my mother's memories, but by the time she came back to England she was consumed by her present, and her past was a kind of no man's land.

When I think of our life together in South Africa I really do feel a huge sense of gratitude and admiration. After first staying with the hospitable and welcoming Marais family in Hout Bay, my mother got work playing in a cocktail bar. She entered the world of interior decoration, working in a shop. She rented a little one-bedroomed flat near a school called Herschel, in Claremont, a suburb of Cape Town, where I went and received an excellent education. And where I made two lifelong friends: Pamela Baker, sadly no longer with us; and Jackie Jeppe. Later in life Pamela, having qualified as a lawyer, went to live in Hong Kong to work in a law practice but, eventually, started her own firm specialising in providing legal help for the Vietnamese Boat People. She was a kind of saviour, filled with passion and commitment. Cancer extinguished her flame far too early.

I wasn't long at Herschel before my mother was offered a job in Johannesburg, playing the piano at The Orange Grove Hotel. So, we went north and I had to move to St Mary's Diocesan School for Girls convent in Pretoria as a boarder. I was there for a year and, I must admit, I really liked the nuns and their way of life. The sense of security and serenity appealed to me. But, once again, I was off south, back to Cape Town and this time my mother had rented a thatched cottage in a different suburb, Newlands. The garden contained a guava tree, a cherry guava tree and Cape gooseberries grew along the fence. Apart from that it was a fairly wild garden with a stream at the bottom, a wonderful playground for anyone with imagination.

The best thing was that we had dogs. Blitzy, a wire-haired terrier, and Peter, a Doberman. He was our guard dog. We needed a good guard dog as one day, we returned home, found the front door open and, as we walked in, a huge man came hurtling down the stairs shouting at us. He rushed out of the door and we ran upstairs, pretty shaken, to find all my mother's clothes and jewellery heaped onto sheets and a bedspread, which were spread out on the floor. So, Peter joined the family.

When Blitzy died, I was inconsolable. I desperately needed a little dog to love and look after. So we found Simon, a six week old black cocker spaniel. Sweet and shy, he was everything to me.

MY MOTHER continued her cabaret and cocktail piano playing, and my great friend at home was Ethel Maquenukana. She was a cook, housekeeper and just about the kindest person you could find. When my mother remarried, and Ethel suddenly had three extra people to look after, she took it all in her stride.

My stepfather, Jack Rudd, had two children from his first marriage. Gillian and William. It was quite strange having a stepsister and stepbrother and they probably felt the same. Gill and I had to share a bedroom as the cottage wasn't that big, but it worked well and we all got on. Thanks, I believe, to my stepfather who was sympathetic, sweet-natured and always kind to me. But were we equally kind to him? When the war ended my mother promptly decided that she and I were returning to England. It was very confusing for me and must have been deeply sad for Jack. So from a family of five we were now back to two. It was goodbye to Jack, and Gillian and William, and my dear Ethel and beloved dogs. What agony. So many goodbyes, and so often. Only William and I remain, and we keep in touch from time to time.

When we returned from six years in South Africa, I went back to the same boarding school, Heron's Ghyll, and, for a while, lived with Phyllis and the kind family she worked for. The boarding school, near Horsham, had changed little since I left six years earlier. But I now had grown up a little, developing an interest in words and poetry. This was soon to include acting.

The school was well known for the open-air floodlit productions of Shakespeare plays it put on in the summer – under a huge copper beech tree. My first role was Theseus in *A Midsummer Night's Dream*, for which I sported a sort of tunic and some cross-garters up my calf – with another around my head! A year later I progressed to Ariel in *The Tempest* – a rather plump one I seem to remember. I was to be in the same play many years later on the radio – playing Miranda to John Gielgud's Prospero. Last of all was *A Winter's Tale*, acting the part of Paulina. How could I, as a schoolgirl, have known that only four years later I would be acting in that same play on the London stage, in the celebrated production by Peter Brook?

Eventually my mother found a little house in Knightsbridge and I went back to live with her. She still worked as a musician, playing at Quaglino's and The Allegro in Bury Street at cocktail time. She was a great attraction. Her playing was exceptionally beautiful and melodic – and she was a charming and attractive personality.

Some years later she met up with an old friend, Sir Charles Oakeley – a sort of 'Stagedoor Johnny' (as they were called!) from the Savoy and Berkeley days before the war. He was a delightful man, they got on well, and they married! Bill and I were their witnesses. My mother gave up her career and went to live with Charles at his home in Frittenden in Kent. Tragically, it was to last only a few years as he died of cancer and my mother became a widow.

I said before that my father suffered from poor health. When I was grown up my mother confessed that he also had a drink problem. It was probably stupid of me but I didn't really want to hear it, to know about it. He died when I was 17 and I felt it wasn't fair that he couldn't tell me his side of the story. He died in 1949, when he was only 53. In his obituary, my great-uncle Stephen McKenna wrote: 'Enviably endowed with almost every other gift, Terry McKenna was denied the greatest of all: a robust constitution. He had more than his fair share of illness; and those who loved him the most will the least begrudge him now the rest for which he yearned increasingly'. Reading this again, after so many years, I feel an overwhelming sense of guilt – shame really, that I had not known enough about it or been able to be of some small comfort at what must have been a pitiful end.

I never saw my father enough to feel totally at ease with him, something I have always regretted. But girls in mid-teens in the 1940s were very naïve compared with today (well, I certainly was) and I would never have dared to suggest we met. In the war he was an ARP warden and met and married Gladys, who drove ambulances. I remember she made delicious chocolate cake whenever I visited them from school.

My father was married three times but none of the marriages lasted. Gladys always remained a dear friend and I believe she and my father still loved each other even when they were no longer together. Before she died she gave me a packet of letters that had passed between them. To be honest, I can hardly bear to think about him dying. Really alone. You can love people but not be able to live with them. Both my parents were sad and alone when they died. If only – if only –

In two days' time it is the anniversary of my mother's death. I have put hyacinths on her grave. Something that will last a while.

SOMETIMES I feel very quiet. In a quiet space. It's almost like a time of preparation. Sorting out the cupboards, the photo albums, the papers, making sure everything is in order. I hope I won't die quite yet but you never know. I still keep rushing round the world so anything could happen! 'At your age,' they say, 'what energy!'. Well, it does flag periodically but when you have curiosity and purpose you're not ready to come to a halt. When the moment comes to 'shuffle off…etc', what I shall most miss will be seeing my grandchildren, all nine of them, grow, grow up, fulfil their dreams, make my children grandparents. I don't expect I shall become a great-grandmother as my eldest grandchild is only 19. But who knows?

I do wish Bill could have met all these gorgeous, energetic spirits – so sweet and funny and endearing and talented. All different. As are our four.

Bill was a Geordie and came from a large family. He was one of five children. The aunties, cousins, nephews and nieces stretch endlessly out on the family tree. Although 'my' tree is big with shoots and branches to right and left, our actual branch is more like a twig. I am an only child with one cousin, Johnny. I think this is why I always wanted lots of children. How lucky I have been.

The King and I

ALTHOUGH I COULD NEVER call myself a musician, I suppose I have inherited a love of music from my mother and her family – a need for it really – and I can sing in tune. When I was a drama student, I went to Maestro Georges Cunelli at the Wigmore Hall Studios for singing lessons. He was a great teacher and I did my best with 'O Mio Babbino Caro', raising false hopes that I might one day be a real singer. But, to his disappointment, my heart wasn't really in it. Although I continued sporadically to take lessons and maintained my friendship with the Maestro and his assistant, Marjorie Russell, my life went in a different direction. Even so, I always believed his training was invaluable in the singing roles I was to attempt later on.

As an actress I never dreamed I'd be in musicals – but as an actress who sang rather than a singer who acted, I had the most glorious experiences in musical theatre – from *The Beggar's Opera* with the Royal Shakespeare Company, to *A Little Night Music*, *The King and I* and *Winnie*. The last, with Robert Hardy, the definitive interpreter of Winston Churchill, was a flop and my last job in the theatre in 1988. I made a couple of long-playing records – one of my songs in *The King and I* and a collection of love songs called 'Two Faces of Love'. My sister-in-law, Linden, did a pencil drawing of me for the cover, which Bill loved. And, although I was never a particularly talented singer, I don't think I was ever happier as a performer than when I was in a musical atmosphere. Nothing gets the adrenaline surging or the spirit flying higher than hearing the orchestra playing the overture. *The King and I*, from 1979, has to be the highlight for me.

The fact that Yul Brynner himself was to be the 'King', and that it was being staged at the London Palladium, meant that the number of actresses trying for the part of Mrs Anna was staggering. By the time I reached audition number three there was a shortlist of three or four. I remember feeling more and more nervous. This audition was to be in New York, in a theatre, with an audience consisting of Yul Brynner, Billy Hammerstein, son of the lyricist Oscar, and Richard Rodgers the composer. With me was one of the producers, Ross Taylor

Above left: As Desirée in A Little Night Music.
Above right: With Yul Brynner at the press conference to announce 'Mrs Anna' in The King and I.
Below: As Anna in The King and I, *teaching the King's children.*

as well as John Taylor, a brilliant accompanist who had coached me patiently in the songs. Arriving in New York, we were informed that the audition was not to be in a theatre but in Rodgers' apartment. The famous 'audience' would not be invisible in the anonymous darkness of a theatre but bathed in daylight sitting on sofas and chairs less than a stone's throw away! I don't know if you can imagine what I felt. Of course everyone was considerate and made me feel welcome, but I felt less than confident, trying not to bump into coffee tables as I went through Mrs Anna's songs. The audition over, Rodgers asked me to take one of the songs up a key - alarming to say the least - and then, finally, we had coffee and looked out at the New York rooftops. I remember nothing more except going to see *The King and I* that evening. Hard to believe, watching Brynner command the stage, that he had to audition to play the part of the King opposite Gertrude Lawrence in 1951. So he, too, must have known what it was like awaiting the result!

After the show we were all taken to dinner, driven in Brynner's limousine with blacked-out windows. It was parked inside the theatre building - a consequence of an incident some time before when someone had tried to attack Brynner outside the theatre. I never discovered why.

The fantasy few days in New York ended and I went home, longing to be back with the family, and unsure of how long I would have to wait until I knew the news about the audition. It was six weeks.

Ross Taylor had decided to stage the press call to announce who would play Mrs Anna in an extraordinary and brilliantly theatrical way. The ball gown in which Mrs Anna danced the polka was designed and made, hair and makeup decided on and - Brynner himself flew in from New York. I had to stand at the back of the stage with my back to the auditorium - bustling with press and photographers - and, as the lights went up and the music played, I walked down to the front to be met by Brynner. My heart was racing. I was taking the first steps of the next seventeen months.

So many people have asked me what Brynner was like. Well, he was 'The King'. In the theatre in England I have always felt that the 'company' was the most important ingredient in the mixing bowl of actors and script, rehearsal and performance. The feeling of family. Yul came, I suppose, from a very different tradition - the star system - which here we still seem to hold at arm's length, in the theatre at least.

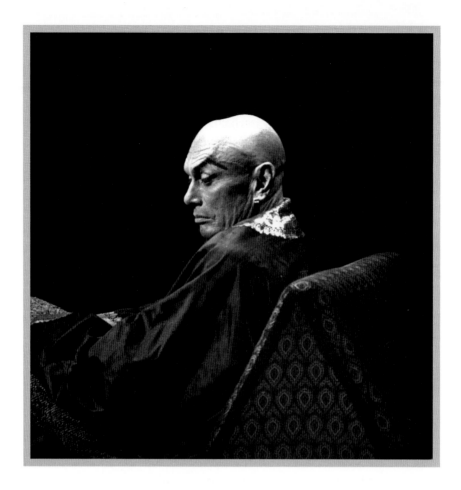

And, after all, he had played the part for many years and countless actresses had been 'Mrs Anna'. He did keep himself distant from the company, and I felt quite sorry about this as he missed a lot of the fun. I can't count the number of children's birthday parties I went to in the big dressing room upstairs, between the shows on matinee days! Such sweet, lovely children in the cast.

Brynner was a very courteous and professional actor and I think we worked well together. I admired him for the way he dealt with pain and never gave in. In his youth he had been a trapeze artist in the circus. He had a serious accident one day when he fell and the safety net was not securely fixed. He was badly injured and these injuries left their legacy. Sometimes his cramp was so painful he could only dance the polka on one leg. He would whisper this to me as we started our twirling and I tried to help by swishing my huge skirt round more vigorously so nothing would be noticed. One thing he could

Virginia McKenna

not tolerate was whistling in the theatre – I was told that the man who had been fixing the safety net in the circus had been whistling while he worked. In rehearsal, on one occasion, we heard someone whistling somewhere above us and Brynner called everything to a halt until the person was found and asked to stop.

It was a happy cast. Apart from the children, there was my old friend from drama school, John Bennett, Paul Williamson and Hye-Young Choi ('Lady Thiang') who became good friends. Dear John is no longer with us, but I still exchange cards and notes with the others. And, of course, there were the brilliant dancers, and the real singers, June Angela and Marty Rhone.

I can't write these few words about one of the most wonderful theatrical experiences of my life without mentioning two more people. The musical director Cyril Ornadel and Tony Stenson, who took over the baton when Cyril left. Cyril's expertise as a conductor was unequalled. He was the most sensitive and wise teacher, helping me to understand how to sustain the demanding speaking and singing role of Mrs Anna for three-hour performances, eight times a week. I remember him telling me that the words mattered most. The story, just sung, not spoken.

Tony was younger but inspired equal confidence. I always recall one evening when I was halfway through a song known as the 'soliloquy'. Suddenly I 'dried'. I couldn't for the life of me remember the next words I should sing. The orchestra was playing along and Tony waving his baton. There was no way I could stop, so I made up a few words of total nonsense and just kept going until I managed to return to the script. I saw Tony lift his eyes from the score. His eyebrows practically disappeared into his hairline and his mouth fell open in astonishment! I could only pray he was the only person who noticed! It is a special joy that Tony and his partner Jenny and I have met again – only last year.

The management of *The King and I* ran a very professional ship. Every aspect was maintained to a very high standard and, I believe, this was why it was as fresh and clean on the last night as it was on the first. Sixteen months is a long time to be in a show. Friendships and loyalties are formed and, inevitably, there is sadness when the time comes to say goodbye. I had been asked if I would go to the USA and tour the show with Brynner. It was a huge compliment. But I wanted to return to my family who had helped me so much for so long. I came home with a happy heart.

Everyone in the theatre knows how the exigencies of long runs or tours or films on location can put a strain on family life. I was always conscious of how generous Bill and my children were when work came up which was irresistible. 'You must do it – we'll work things out.' Bill and I always believed it was important to understand each other's needs for self-expression. And not only as actors. Sometimes Bill would go to Sardinia to write, walk, think, be quiet. That was his nature. He thought deeply, wrote profoundly, had ideas years ahead of his time. And he painted wonderful little pictures of the sea, dotted with boats, framed in the wooden posts and canopy of our big terrace. Sometimes I would find his artistic 'notes' between the pages of a book he had been reading. Such poignant treasures.

Virginia McKenna

I Return to Africa

2007

I T IS OVER ONE and a half years since I wrote anything for this book. Now I'm 75. I haven't wanted to – have been too busy travelling, working, just living life. But today, November 3rd, in an aeroplane on my way to South Africa, I suddenly felt the need to take up my pen again.

In 1962 when Bill was at Stratford for a season with the Royal Shakespeare Company, his agent – Monty Mackay – mentioned an enquiry for him (and me) regarding a proposed film, *Born Free*, based on Joy Adamson's famous book. There was an initial meeting and then Bill went on to do other work – *Lorna Doone*, for the BBC, *A Giant is Born* for US Heritage TV, in which he played President Andrew Jackson, and then a play on Broadway, *Abraham Cochrane*. I flew out for the first night. Unfortunately it was also the last night! The press was unanimously scathing. In those days the American public was exceptionally influenced by the 'notices' (I don't know if it is different now), and as shows were hugely expensive to put on no-one could take a gamble on this one. So it closed.

It was quite a blow. To recover, Bill and I took a short holiday with the producer Helen Jacobson and her husband. Bill began to wonder if anything was happening about *Born Free*. He contacted Monty, who told us that the producers had just been in touch and wanted to meet us. Two weeks later we were having tea at the Mayfair Hotel with Paul Radin, one of the producers, and Tom McGowan, who was then the director. I hadn't read the book, so I rushed to buy a copy on our return from America. It was a remarkable story. Paul and Tom enthused about the film and the lions. 'Oh, they're just like big pussycats. You can just let them come up to you and you can stroke them.' We listened, and nodded, and wondered.

Then: 'Will you do it?'

'Yes,' we both replied without hesitation. The challenge, the adventure, was irresistible. Out in the street we jumped for joy like two kids!

The executive producer was Carl Foreman, famous as the script-writer of *High Noon* and writer/producer of *MacKenna's Gold* and *Young Winston*. (He also wrote the script for *Born Free* but under a pseudonym.) We were just actors, invited to play the parts of Joy and her husband, George. We never imagined that sharing ten and a half months with lions, a film crew and living in an old settlers' house in the bush at Naro Moru with our children, 125 miles north of Nairobi, would develop into a life-changing experience. It was a challenging film to make – we were breaking new ground, as when the two former circus lionesses originally chosen to play the part of Elsa proved too dangerous, we found ourselves learning to develop friendship and trust with a variety of other lions. Each came with his or her own story, their own individuality, but they shared two things in common. They were not trained animals. And they were fascinating.

We had many, many lessons to learn, but we were blessed to share this period of our life with one of the most remarkable, wise, intuitive, modest and special men we had ever met. George Adamson guided us in his quiet, unassuming way through the difficulties of blending the demands of the film schedule together with the need to develop even closer bonds with our lion friends. No lion is ever really 'tame'. After centuries of domestication cats still hunt birds and mice, so why should a first, second or even third generation captive lion be any different?

Suffice it to say that our safety was built on mutual trust and on the hours we spent with the animals to achieve it. The dawn walks on the cobwebbed plains, the lunchtime picnics, the moments of shared rest in the enclosures – time was the secret.

I remember still the agony of saying goodbye to our 'Elsas'. Most of them were being sold to zoos and safari parks, which had been a bone of contention between the Adamsons and ourselves on one hand – and the producers on the other. Three of them, Boy, Girl and Ugas, were given to George to return to the wild and, filming over, he took them up to the Meru Reserve, north-east of Mount Kenya, where he set up a camp. A new life began for all of them. And for us.

When I return to Africa
It is with friends.
Friends from other journeys,
Other times.
Our hearts beat as one
Seeing mountains
With the same eyes
Smelling sun-baked earth
With the same joy
Our minds opening
In the same way
To new people
Strange encounters
Deep feelings.
Africa binds us.
Inexplicably.

What lies beyond the hill?
Do thorn trees shade
Those mammoth giants?
Will starlings so superb greet
Our wide gaze
As myriad images of nature
Crowd the scene?
This land so old and yet
So full of birth
This land where life began.
How poignant is its skein
Around our hearts.

Dew – damp cobwebs
Thread the dawn grass
Cry of fish eagle
Roar of lion
Call of hyaena
Pierce the air
Haunting our souls forever.

Friendship around the fire
Burns deep.
Beneath the night's dark ceiling
Daisied with stars
We talk and smile.
And share the silence.
Remembering the day.

IN 2006 I went with a small group of friends to Meru. We revisited Elsa's Kopje (hill), an almost secret hideaway, so carefully designed, so unobtrusive, you might never know it was there. It blended into the landscape so well it might have passed for just one of Meru's hills. But this one overlooked the site of George's old camp. I walked around the spot where his simple cluster of huts used to be and found little relics of that time still on the ground. Bits of metal, hub of a wheel. In the warm air birds sang sweetly and I suddenly felt bereft. There are so many moments I have wanted to share with Bill since he died over

1968: Reunion with George and Ugas the lion.

▶   *Virginia McKenna*

twelve years ago, and this was one of them. Hey ho. *C'est la vie.* And all that.

George's rehabilitation of Ugas, Boy and Girl was controversial but, for two of the lions, successful. Joy set up a separate camp in Meru dedicated to her work with cheetah. Bill came to Meru to do his first film as a wildlife documentary maker, *The Lions Are Free*, taking the first steps on a path that would eventually lead us both into a new world. It all seemed very positive and Bill was quite unprepared for the metaphorical dust-devil that suddenly swirled down and enveloped him. His film was about George's work – a follow-up if you like to the feature film. He invited Joy to be a part of it, but not so strongly featured, for obvious reasons. Her work was with cheetah. She could not understand this, and could not forgive him. I was deeply shocked. I couldn't believe, after all we had gone through together, that anything could break our friendship. It was tough and sad. But, ever the optimist, I seized on the opportunity of another visit to Meru in 1968 to try and bring us together again.

We were making a film called *An Elephant Called Slowly* and Bill wanted to include George in some way. So we went to his camp. It was heaven for me. Seeing him and Ugas and Girl (Boy was off somewhere) surrounded by wilderness, enveloped by Africa's warm arms and discovering that the trust we had established with the lions was unbroken.

I recall saying that we couldn't leave without seeing Joy, so we set off in the Land Rover to where George said she took her evening walk. Suddenly I saw her striding through the bush. I jumped out and ran after her, calling her name. She didn't stop straight away, but finally we met and I gave her a big hug. I asked her to come with me to see Bill and to please let's start again as it was all so pointless. Looking at her I felt her strength, her reluctance to give in, but I clung to the small chance that she would open her heart. It was not to be. They shook hands, greeted each other and then she said – in so many words – that we could start again if Bill apologised. He agreed he would, if he knew what it was for. And that was it. Joy invited me back to her camp, but not Bill. I told her this was obviously out of the question. So, in silence, we drove her back. It was heartbreaking and I have never really put it to rest. Some years later Joy asked Bill if he would let her have some cheetah footage which had been filmed up at Meru. He gave it to her without question.

George, myself, Bill – our reunion with Girl.

It is always disturbing to retain negative thoughts about people – especially those you have admired, loved or been friends with. The little canker grows until, almost without realising it, it has developed into the only way you remember someone.

For a while, because I thought Joy had treated Bill unjustly, I continued to be angry and resentful. But what good did that do? None. I consciously started to think about her in a positive way. I tried to understand her angers, resentments and jealousies and put them into context; to restore her talents, her dedication to wild animals and their survival in the wild, her courage in the face of physical pain to the top of my memory box. And I have succeeded. In a way I realise now how lonely she must have felt. It is true she sometimes alienated people and made enemies, but she was a victim of that aspect of her nature, and that was truly sad.

How could I not count as one of my most extraordinary and treasured experiences the three days she and I spent alone in Meru, Elsa's home? I had finished filming, but Bill had a few more days' work and Joy invited me to go to Meru, where she would share her memories with me.

We lived simply in her camp. We bathed in 'Elsa's' river, climbed Elsa's rock, lingered by Elsa's grave and I felt the depth of Joy's emotions as she talked about her extraordinary years with her leonine friend. It was as if she mourned the death of her child. In a way that was the truth. Her love for Elsa was unequivocal, total, unconditional. As is one's love for one's children.

I think it must have been very difficult for Joy to stand by and watch someone else 'playing' her. Not that she ever made me feel that as she was always helpful and generous with her responses to my questions, 'what was it like?', 'how did you feel?'.

So - these are the positive memories I keep and I know Bill and George would be glad of that.

⌣

WHO COULD have imagined that thirty-eight years later, in 2006, I would travel with my group of friends to 'Joy's Camp' in the Shaba Reserve. I was much looking forward to seeing this new camp, established in Joy's memory, and it lived up to all my expectations. It was here that she released Penny, the leopard, into the wild. An amazing story, wonderfully told in her book Queen of Shaba. And here where she was brutally murdered in 1980, on January 3rd. Bill's birthday. It was tragic, shocking and deeply upsetting for all who knew her. To my knowledge, her murderer (who had been on her staff) is still in prison. He was accused of stealing valuable personal items belonging to Joy. Profoundly insulted, he returned to camp and took his revenge. The initial story was that she had been killed by lions. The knife wound told a different story.

Now Joy's Camp is serene. It has a remote beauty that one yearns for in our crowded lives. The rooms for the guests are exquisitely yet simply designed (by Lesley-Anne Rowley who designed Elsa's Kopje), the welcome as warm as anywhere in Kenya, the wild animals living peacefully. And adding to its unique element is the memory of an extraordinary, courageous, passionate woman who, according to Desmond Morris, 'had made people start to query the morality of keeping animals in captivity - in zoos and, even more so, in circuses.

The essence of Elsa's story was her freedom and that was something that zoos and circuses were sadly lacking.' Morris wrote that Joy had 'achieved the difficult goal of not merely providing a passing entertainment, but of actually shifting public feelings towards an animal species. Elsa the lioness had become an ambassador for her kind.'

In front of the camp is a natural spring, where a colourful and varied crowd of animals come to drink. But we were not only here to experience the wildlife. We were about to have a very special meeting.

Some years ago a young Czech woman, Zuzana Beranova, who had become deeply interested in Joy and her life and was awakening Joy's memory back in her original homeland (now the Czech Republic), had come to Kenya and visited all the places where Joy had lived. She met many of the people who had known her. So, naturally, she came to Shaba.

One of those she met was Mohammed Tubi, the Mzee, who had worked for Joy in her camp until her death. Through Zuzana, and helped by the manager at Joy's Camp, I was able to find the Mzee and invite him to come and meet us. He travelled for a day on foot, with his son and an elder from his village. Only from the Park gate did he get a ride. We all met in the lounge area, in the early evening, joined by the Assistant Warden, and it was a touching and delightful time. With help from people who translated we talked for about an hour and planned our safari out into the Park the next morning.

We met at 7.30 am and drove out in the warm, early light to the rocky area where Penny gave birth to her cubs. The Mzee showed us where he and Joy used to bring meat for Penny and where, later, the cubs used to come down with their mother and play. It was such a privilege to be with this man who had been a part of Joy's life and who was happy to share his memories with us. Why did I want to meet this old man, to go to Joy's Camp where her life came to an end? In a way it was bringing things full circle. Ending one of the chapters. Laying some things to rest.

The morning ended with us all breakfasting under some trees, and with us giving tokens of our appreciation to Mohammed, his son and the village elder. His smile was all.

Pole Pole and the Birth of Zoo Check

I'M UNCERTAIN WHAT WORDS to write down next. There are so many paths to follow – our children and their children, Bill's documentaries, the melting Arctic, the horrors of Iraq, the beauty of our little woodland – ablaze with bluebells in the spring. But perhaps those are for later. Now I've written the words *An Elephant Called Slowly* the fierce feelings of that story – the story of Pole Pole, the tragic little elephant whose death was to catapult us into the rest of our life – can't be held back.

NINETEEN SIXTY-EIGHT. Back to Kenya with James Hill (who had directed *Born Free*) to make *An Elephant Called Slowly*, a little film comedy about elephants. We were to work with Simon Trevor, the cameraman famous for his wildlife films, and to stay in some bandas in Tsavo National Park where David and Daphne Sheldrick lived. David was Senior Game Warden of the Park and Daphne had already begun her world-renowned work of rescuing and nurturing orphaned animals. Especially elephants.

When we arrived in Tsavo we found Daphne had three elephants she was caring for, but no little two year old – which is what we needed for the film. Suddenly we heard that a young elephant had been captured from the wild and was being held in the trapper's yard in Nairobi. She was to be a gift from the government to London Zoo.

We watched her rushing around the small stockade, disoriented and fearful, and we had serious misgivings about subjecting her to yet another potentially stressful experience. David reassured us. I've always believed that he and Daphne were to elephants what George was to lions. And, of course, to this day Daphne continues to rescue and care for little orphaned eles at her orphanage outside Nairobi. Thanks to her wise expertise most eventually return to the wild.

Sure enough, within a few days the elephant, Pole Pole (pronounced *Poleh, Poleh* – 'Slowly, slowly' in Swahili), was calm. She began to trust us and follow us and a sweet friendship developed. And we got to know a very large rhino, thanks to some 'Sugar Daddies'! In Tsavo there were two rhinos that had been rehabilitated back to the wild by the Shel-

Above: Bill and I walking with Pole Pole in An Elephant Called Slowly.

Right: Pole Pole touching heads with David Sheldrick, Senior Game Warden of Tsavo National Park, Kenya.

Below: Bill and I feed 'Sugar Daddies' to Ruedi the rhino.

Virginia McKenna

Top left: Pole Pole collapses in the crate, 1983.

Above and left: In the elephant enclosure at London Zoo in 1982.

Below: Pole Pole recognises us at the zoo in 1982.

dricks, but which still enjoyed the company of human friends. I had heard that Rufus and Ruedi were crazy about Sugar Daddies – a sort of toffee lollipop on a stick – so I went into Woolworths in Nairobi and bought the entire supply, to the astonishment of the saleslady behind the counter! And it was true. The look of ecstasy on the rhinos' faces as they sucked and devoured the lollipops – stick and all – was a sight to remember.

We worked for six weeks on the film, every waking hour with the elephants and developing a very special friendship with Pole Pole. The storyline of the film was a simple one. A young couple had been invited to Kenya by a friend who was going into hospital for an operation. He asked them, in his absence, to look after some friends at his house miles from Nairobi in the African bush.

The battered old windscreen-less Land Rover that the couple hired finally ended the bone-shattering journey when they 'ran out of road' – at their friend's house. They then discovered that the friends were, in fact, a little group of elephants!

How to look after them, what food to give them, what kind of mud they liked to wallow in, plus the various excitements and challenges of living out in the wild created a delightful story (initially made for children) whilst, at the same time, providing genuine information about the life of a wild elephant and what it needs to lead a fulfilled and happy one.

But, inevitably, the joyous time of filming and sharing our days with Pole Pole ended and the moment we had been dreading arrived.

The authorities agreed to our request to buy Pole Pole so that she could remain with the Sheldricks' little group of orphans, but they told us another baby would have to be caught. The gift for London Zoo must be honoured. Sick at heart, we couldn't condone a second horror story for another elephant family, and so Pole Pole came to London Zoo. Bill went to see her (I couldn't face the ordeal). He took some oranges and, of course, she recognised him. It was heartbreaking. From the African bush to the barren elephant compound at the zoo is a gigantic leap of body and mind. What could be going through hers? Bill decided not to go again – she had to adjust somehow to her new 'home', bonding with her elephant companions and her keepers. We were helpless.

Fifteen years later she was dead. In 1982 Daphne had written to us and told us she had heard Pole Pole was to be destroyed. What had gone wrong? What was happening? Why kill a 'teenager'? We contacted Brian Jackman, the highly respected travel writer and journalist – then working for the *Sunday Times* – and visited the zoo with him. As we approached her compound she was led away inside. Out of sight. A strange coincidence?

This didn't prevent Brian writing a feature about her – a story taken up next day by the *Daily Mail*. What did we learn? That Pole Pole's companions had been sent to other zoos or had died, that all that remained of her tusks was one broken stump, that she had become 'difficult' and was a problem. Well, how could it be otherwise? No touching, no family, no communication – hell on earth for female elephants. And stored away in that deep memory was the time we had lived with her in Tsavo, in Kenya.

Again we went to see her. This time with the *Daily Mail* photographer. We watched her pace her lonely, repetitive path to and fro in front of the elephant house, and then we called her name. *Pole Pole.* She stopped. She turned towards us. She walked to the edge of the moat and extended her trunk towards our outstretched hands. It was an agony I feel to this day. She still recognised us. That recognition, was it forgiveness? Forgiving ourselves was another matter.

And so began our attempt to 'rescue' her. I found a wildlife reserve in South Africa who agreed to take her, and someone to be in charge of her rehabilitation. A suggestion categorically turned down by the zoo authorities. I imagine we became a thorn in their side as we desperately tried to find a way to help her. Finally they agreed to move her to Whipsnade – more space, elephant companions. Although a compromise it was better than London. It was not to be. Kept in her travelling crate for many hours, she collapsed and had to be jacked up onto her feet. A week later she was anaesthetised to examine an injured leg. Then – 'she lost the will to live', they said. And they ended it.

The following year we launched our little organisation, Zoo Check. We believed with a passion I keep to this day that her death must have a purpose. Out of her last breath must spring a new life – we must try and do something for so many other animals which endure pitiful captive conditions. And not only elephants. We must look at them, film them, talk about them, gather to us people who felt the same concerns, as well as experts who could endorse our more emotional and instinctive perspective with scientific observations. We didn't question, for one moment, that this was what we had to do. Our life changed forever.

During our months of struggle to try and help Pole Pole we had been contacted by many people who had read the press articles and who had wanted to support our efforts to return her to Africa. We wrote to them and asked them if they could help us to start a small organisation called Zoo Check, inspired by her tragic death.

Zoo Check (in 1991 renamed The Born Free Foundation) held its press launch on March 19th 1984, supported by that most generous-hearted, compassionate and loyal of friends, Joanna Lumley. Our Founder Patron.

It was lucky we went into this with our eyes open as we became the target of biting scorn and criticism from all levels of people involved in the zoo community. They ridiculed us for our lack of scientific knowledge, our emotions. In fact we and our co-founders of Zoo Check (which included our eldest son Will) were described as a bunch of emotional cranks and it was said that our organisation would be a nine-day wonder. Did they really believe that would intimidate us? How little they understood. We had taken on a challenge, espoused a cause that no-one could destroy. We are still here in 2007, twenty-three years later.

Virginia McKenna

Bill

THE SPIRIT OF ADVENTURE and dedication to a cause must, I'm sure, be in my genes. The willingness to take on challenges single-mindedly. My great-uncle Reginald McKenna held a bewildering number of positions in the Liberal government of his day as well as that of Chairman of the Midland Bank for over twenty-five years. Sadly, I did not meet him or inherit his financial brilliance, but I am glad to say it is still alive and well in one of my children and grandchildren. My great-grandfather Sir Morell Mackenzie was an eminent surgeon, operating on many famous actors, actresses and writers – including Ellen Terry, Henry Irving, Arthur Wing Pinero, Beerbohm Tree and Harry Kemble and I have a silver punch-bowl presented to him in gratitude by the group of 'players', left to me by Emily, the widow of Uncle Gerald, my father's eldest brother, on her death. I have always felt that surgery of any kind is a huge challenge – you hold someone's life in your hands, sometimes against all the odds, and what greater commitment can there be than that? Yes, commitment is the key. As for Bill – well, so much of his young adulthood was spent facing danger, taking risks, putting himself last. I wish that he was here to talk things through.

I never wanted to live with anyone but him. Soon he will have been gone fourteen years. But he is always there with me and he knows I am fine on my own. In fact I need to be. I must have space and solitude to remember and cherish all those people I love. Those who have gone and those who still bring joy to my life. And, in writing this, I can re-awaken some memories of moments that enrich my old age. The sad and difficult memories too. It's important not to bury those too deep. They make you what you are. A whole person.

We have an old pine settle in the dining room and the wood on its back has darkened where the body of our dog, Sarda, leaned against it. And at the bottom of the stairs leading down from Bill's studio the wood next to the door is deep brown from where his hand touched it before opening it. My hand touches it now. Perhaps it will soon be black. I never feel lonely, or frightened, and I have a deep and unshakeable love for my family home. It is my dearest wish that it

will somehow stay in our family when I am gone. It is a corner of paradise - watching the birds, hearing the owls at night, meeting a deer on the path through the woods, seeing the grandchildren balancing on the long, low branches of the ancient beech tree, pretending, with a stick, to fish in the bottom pond.

As the world becomes increasingly chaotic, as more people are senselessly killed, as religions incite more hatred and distrust, as order breaks down in spite of governments' frantic but crazy attempts to make new rules and pass more laws, my hillside haven survives as a breath of sanity and beauty. Over the years many people have come to our house and said what a lovely atmosphere it has. The greatest compliment I could ever receive.

After thirteen and a half years without Bill some days are really difficult - especially the evenings. When I see two old people walking down the street holding hands it is almost unbearable. I know what that is like. Bill had the warmest, kindest, most reassuring hands. Just now I'd like to sit with him and see if he would talk a little about the war. He rarely did and never went to any reunions. He kept in touch with just a few of his colleagues of whom he was very fond and with whom he had strong ties of shared experiences.

Virginia McKenna

He joined the Royal Northumberland Fusiliers in 1940 (adding a year onto his age so he would be accepted). He was commissioned in 1941 and joined the 4/9 Gurkha Rifles in 1942. Later, in 1944, serving under General Wingate in the Second Chindit Campaign, he was wounded and struck down with malaria but returned to work with Force 136. Now as a Major. I knew, from the stories he sometimes told me by the fire on winter evenings, of the horrors he saw, the agony of seeing comrades killed or wounded, the kindness of villagers in the dangerous areas they were fighting behind enemy lines in Burma. Of the particular menace and atmosphere of hidden danger that is part of warfare in a jungle. He stayed in the Far East until 1947 and then came home to begin life as a struggling actor, sharing a basement flat in Chelsea with his friend and fellow actor Anthony Steel, and living on a diet of cauliflower cheese.

Because of his knowledge of that part of the world, Bill was sent as a member of a small investigation team into Hiroshima - after the atom bomb had been dropped. I have his handwritten account of that terrible experience. It is in a small leather-bound 'Year-by-Year' diary, and is one of my most treasured and loved memories of him as it reveals the extraordinary extent of his compassion and forgiveness.

I have walked in Hiroshima now. It is the biggest cemetery in the world. Its a place where everything died at once; men, women, children, flowers, trees, every piece of wood and bricks. The place disintegrated; there were no holes. Bricks became dust. Trees became blackened stubs. Bottles melted and assumed grotesque shapes. Pieces of metal curled and folded like silk. There were no rags or pieces of paper; those and wooden beams and planks had disappeared as completely as the flowers and human beings who lived there... I should have enough hatred of the Japanese after the last few years to be able to justify the bombing, enough at least to satisfy my conscience. There is no justification for this bombing. Had we lost a hundred thousand more men, and I would have gladly been among them, Japan would have been beaten to her knees, as was Germany... In years to come the world will learn that the Jap was forced to surrender, but not defeated.

He wrote this when he was twenty-six. Fighting to save others and to survive yourself. I suppose that is at the heart of most conflicts.

Bill was awarded the MBE but he never used it, never mentioned it. So it is not on his gravestone. What are carved there are the knives, the Gurkha khukris - a reminder of the men he led, cherished and admired so much and who were, to the end, part of his being.

We first met in London in *I Capture the Castle*, the play based on Dodie Smith's delightful book. The cast included Roger Moore, who was whisked away to Hollywood halfway through the run! Bill was married to Patricia Raine and had an adorable little daughter, Anna. I was about to marry Denholm Elliott. I'd first met Denholm when we were in the film of *The Cruel Sea*. He was a fine actor and a delightful person, but I suppose I have to admit that, for both of us, our marriage was a mistake. There were times, of course, when things went well but I knew in my heart it wouldn't work. So I had to leave.

After that it was a kind of wilderness. Eventually Denholm and I met again at the house, and I remember sitting in the kitchen together dividing the gifts we had received between us. It was quite calm, in fact, but sad. I remember that. The good thing is that we met up again some years later, in 1961. Bill was in New York in the stage production of *A Cook for Mr General* - he played a Greek cook and had to dance - 'Grecian style'. (It always made us laugh as he wasn't a natural dancer and always said he had two left feet.) Denholm was also in a play on Broadway and I went along to see a matinee. As always he was brilliant. Bill had suggested he might like to come and have lunch with us one Sunday in Connecticut where we had ensconced ourselves and our two children, William and Louise, and Bill's daughter Anna (her mother was on tour) and our nanny, Muriel Horton. So Denholm came and spent the day - it was a good day.

Certainly, when Denholm and I worked together later in a television play, *The Blue Dress*, in 1983, it was friendly and comfortable and I had the pleasure of meeting his second wife Susie. I recall the three of us having a drink together before dinner. Denholm sat facing us across the table in the bar. He suddenly said: 'This is amazing! I can't believe I'm sitting looking at my two wives!' He died in 1992 and Bill and I went to his memorial service at St James's Piccadilly. Little did I know that I would be there again two years later remembering Bill.

In my heart I think I always felt that Bill and I would be together. The journey was tough and the obstacles daunting, but as time passed we were drawn together. It was inevitable.

Virginia McKenna

Bill worked successfully for many years, mainly in films and on American television, and I think he will always be remembered as 'Geordie'. 'Come away my wee Geordie!' people would call when we were out and he was recognised. His career in films flourished – *Bhowani Junction*, *The Barretts of Wimpole Street*, *The Smallest Show on Earth*, *The Bridal Path* and then, in 1965, *Duel at Diablo* with Sidney Poitier, James Garner and Dennis Weaver.

Out of the blue disaster struck. I was on my last few days of work playing Adela in the BBC TV production of *A Passage to India*, when an international phone call came through and a voice told me there had been a terrible accident and Bill was in hospital. The next days were a kind of nightmare. As soon as I was able I flew out to California and then to Utah, to the location. Bill had broken a leg. A steel pin was inserted in the bone from knee to ankle. The pin had to have an extra piece added as he was so tall. Also he had dislocated a shoulder. The whole business had been pretty shameful. It was the end of the

Bill with Sidney Poitier and Dennis Weaver in Duel at Diablo.

day's 'shooting'. One more shot, they said. This involved a charge by the cavalry (which Bill led) and the Indians, towards each other, along a dry river bed. For some reason this had not been watered down and, as the horses raced along, the dust obscured everything, resulting in a head-on collision between the lead horses. One can imagine the horror for horses and humans – I was told the Indian who crashed into Bill lost a finger – maybe two.

Bill was then flown to Los Angeles to hospital. Far from being treated immediately, he lay on a hospital trolley all night. In America someone has to sign a paper accepting responsibility for payment of treatment. I was told that the representative of the film company who should have done this 'didn't like hospitals', and couldn't come until the morning!

Bill was always very stoic in the face of pain. He never complained or cried out. I remember, in Sardinia once, a fishing hook got caught in one of his fingers – past the barb. He took a stiff whisky and with pliers pulled it right through. The children and I were trembling. He just gritted his teeth.

Bill returned to the set before he was able to walk. Everyone was waiting to complete this section of the film. I was with him all the time. Waiting for the shot he just lay in the baking sun, sweating inside the uniform, until I found an umbrella and held it over him for some shade. Somehow he had to get up on his horse. So they brought in a kind of mechanical hoist and lifted him level with the saddle. He managed it in agony. He did the scene, remembered his lines, never faltered. Then something really wonderful happened. All the crew and other actors spontaneously applauded. In my view the most deserved applause he ever received as an actor.

As I sit in our house writing this, he surrounds me. The colours of nature reflected in the rooms; the glimpse of a tree that he planted outside a window so I could always see something lovely, even on a dank winter day. The little bits of driftwood, his paintings. I'm sure most families have their treasures but I feel especially blessed to be able to still live amongst mine.

Whose is this hand you hold in yours?
It's yours.

Whose is the smile reflecting yours?
It's yours.

Whose are the eyes that meet your own.
The dreams you dream, the joys you've known,
The sadness you have never shown?
All yours.

In darkest hour, and brightest sun,
In morning light, when day is done,
Since first we met, we two are one.

For everything that's mine
Is yours.

BILL WAS once asked to write his autobiography but he said he hadn't time. He was too busy living. He was an amazing storyteller. His chapter in a book we did in 1987, *Beyond the Bars* was, I think, quite unique. It was the story of Pole Pole, told by herself. Anthropomorphic? Well, purists might say so, but understanding more - as we do now - about the character and nature of elephants, I believe he has caught the soul of this young elephant and enveloped us in her memories and her pain in a way that is heartbreaking and extraordinary. So, although he didn't write his autobiography, his writing - and later his scripts for the films and documentaries he made - is quite revealing of the man holding the pen.

Like Bill I write in longhand. I love the physical process of writing, of seeing the shape of words and letters. Although I can - just about - use a computer, I find this way much more involving and personal. More alive.

A week ago today was our fiftieth wedding anniversary. I spent it quietly. Had a walk. Remembering.

Her head was down
Hidden behind the book.
Reading? Sleeping?
Weeping?
He, beside her,
Unaware.
Until her body's messages
Connected
And he turned
Saw
And, tenderly,
Kissed her cheek.
Held her close.

Now how alone I feel
No body next to mine
To feel my tears.
No arms to hold me close
Against the dark.
That's what I miss
The arms. And the kiss.

Growing Up

I T'S STRANGE WHAT YOU remember. In my nursery in Hampstead where I lived with my father there was a little red fire engine on the mantelpiece. How I loved it. And my bus conductor's uniform complete with hat and ticket machine replete with its many coloured tickets. Pink and blue and green and yellow. Oh there was style and imagination in those days – light years away from the nondescript flimsy white paper of today.

Sipping cocoa on Nanny's knee in front of the fire in the winter. Pure joy. And the nightmare of having to recite 'Albert and the Lion' in front of my father's friends. If only the floor could have swallowed me up. My love of poetry grew as I grew older and my wonderful elocution teacher in South Africa encouraged me and helped me along this captivating path. How wonderful it would be to be able to write 'poet' on those endless forms you have to keep filling in when you travel! I never know what to put so I write 'conservationist'. Which I am, but really an animal campaigner at heart. Sometimes I long to chain myself to the railings.

But for which cause? Cruelty to animals? Neglect of old people in care homes? Child abuse? teenage stabbings? Governments ignoring the voice of the people? Burma, Tibet, 'canned hunting'? Bloodshed, bloodshed everywhere.

Tonight the moon is red
Flaming the night sky
What do I see?
A sign? A message?
A fateful omen
Of the blood
So soon to spill
Upon the earth?
Our earth
Our little planet
So loved, so vulnerable,

So tortured.
What is to come?
Mothers, as I am,
Shrieking their pain
As babies, children,
Glorious young men
Waste their red-moon blood
Upon the thirsty soil.

Five years on it hasn't ended - Iraq, Afghanistan, Israel and Palestine, and now Tibet and turmoil in Kenya. Bodies of innocent children destroyed, families shattered by grief. Neighbours consumed by hatred but suffering the same pain and fear. Like so many of us, try as I might I cannot feel any respect for our government leaders. Change is one thing, chaos is another. Poor decisions that have been taken over the past years - to embroil us in battles in faraway lands, to justify torture. Oh for a handful of wise statesmen who would help us regain our sense of fair play, our respect for each other's differences, our affection for 'the old country'.

Hard to say nowadays
What it is to be
British.
Is it the horrors of hooliganism
Football and internet 'grooming'?
Is it Neighbourhood Watch and compassion?
Possibly.
The pastel colours of our race
Now mix with vibrant tones
From other lands.
Wonderful.
To be British is anything and everything.
Probably.
For me though it is the land itself
That stirs my heart. My loyalty.
Our forests, fields, wild coasts
And yes, roses around the door
And washing in the wind.
To be truly British you love your land.
Completely.

Burma

BURMA IS DOMINATING THE airwaves. How will one ever forget the courage of the hundreds and hundreds of monks filling the streets and our television screens as they peacefully make their protest? Their cry for democracy, denied for so many brutal years, can't be silenced and we must help them.

Aung San Suu Kyi is a prisoner in Burma, under house arrest. She has a house to live in, but she understands all too well that she is a captive. Visitors are restricted, her phone line is cut, her post is monitored. She has been under house arrest for thirteen years. She has no free will, she must suppress her instincts; she has no choice, can make no decisions. This beautiful woman with a beautiful and intelligent mind is dominated and controlled by people who rule by fear. Who have no respect or concern for the well-being or feelings of others. Thirteen years. Yet her spirit, her voice (so rarely heard) stir and inspire us more strongly than ever.

She has been a heroine of mine for a long time. I was so moved by her self-sacrifice when her husband was dying here in Britain, ten years ago. She knew that, if she left Burma to be with him, she might never be allowed to return. He understood this was an impossible choice. He knew she must stay in Burma. Now I pray for her safety.

Bill spent a long time in Burma, deep in the jungle behind enemy lines, fighting the Japanese. He developed a deep and enduring fondness for the country and its people – probably the most beautiful in the world he used to tell me. So it was with extra excitement and expectation that we joined a Bales tour in 1978. This was only the second visit by tourists after the country's closure to outside visitors for many years.

I had been in Hong Kong, appearing in a dinner theatre production of *Something's Afoot*, at the Hilton Hotel. With George Cole, Vivienne Martin, Peter Gale and Angela Douglas. The show ended and I flew to Delhi to meet Bill and join up with our travelling companions. India, Thailand, Nepal and Burma were our destinations. Bill's love of the Far East and its people was infectious, and this journey

sowed the seed for the many future adventures we were to experience in those extraordinary and humbling countries.

In Rangoon we stayed in a huge, grey, soulless hotel, the Inya Lake, that had been built by the Russians. Nothing worked properly. No plug in the basin, the loo handle came off and lamps and electric equipment were supplied by a tangle of unprotected flex. In fact, in a couple of places, the wires poked straight into the wall sockets! But we didn't care as we didn't intend to spend much time in the hotel. Our priority was to try and trace an old friend and war-time colleague of Bill's. We enlisted our guide and gave our friend's name and details. Bill went on up to the hotel room with our cases and, just as I was about to follow, I was called to the telephone. It was Bill's friend. He spoke hesitantly. It was strange and I felt it was important he spoke to Bill straight away. When I reached our room they were talking to each other, and I could tell from Bill's expression that all was not well.

Disappointment hardly describes what he felt. His friend said he now 'worked for God' and hadn't time to see us. He said very little but it was plain that he too was profoundly sad not to be able to embrace his old comrade once more. Later that day our guide oddly referred to the phone conversation. All became clear. The line had been tapped. Was Bill's friend was under house arrest?

I've been reading my notes on our 'safari' organised by the Bales travel company. The experience of Burma, at the end of our travels, was in profound contrast to the days we had spent in Nepal, in India and Thailand. The vibrant colours and energies of Bangkok and Delhi and Kathmandu were replaced, at least in Rangoon, by a sad, muted greyness. A city that seemed uncared for - crumbling buildings, peeling paint. 'Only the Shwedagon Pagoda, with the hundreds of temples and shrines - like a temple city - had a life force and a kind of beauty.'

As I put some flowers on one of the shrines a woman came up and beat a bell. This meant she had performed a good deed and when people see her do this they say 'Well done, well done'. I can't wait to leave Rangoon. We fly to Pagan - city of four million temples! Not for the faint-hearted! The Irrawaddy river winds through the countryside, villagers wend their way endlessly to collect water, the children are friendly and beautiful and give us flowers and our spirits lift. Suddenly, from nowhere, comes the sound of music - cymbals and pipes and drums and a kind of xylophone - young people dancing, a succession of bullock carts with flags flying, and carrying huge sacks of rice. For the government! 'This is the way people pay their taxes,' we are told. 'Why are they so happy?' we ask. 'Oh they are happy to pay, they like the government.'

Almost thirty years on, how things have changed. Now, in May 2008, the Irrawaddy Delta is a place of devastation, ruin and death. Floods have no mercy. Nor, it would appear, have Burma's rulers, allowing minimal help to reach the helpless survivors.

I also loved Mandalay. So different from Rangoon. We were surrounded by beauty - the river, the countryside, the temples. We felt a part of the Buddhist way of life. It was tranquil, calming, friendly and, somehow, timeless. But even in these times Burma struggled to feed its people. It had changed from being an exporter of rice to a country which produced barely enough to feed itself. Everything was state controlled. The average wage was £20 a month and a *longe* (a cloth garment similar to a sarong or a kikoy) cost a quarter of the monthly wage.

The countryside was blooming, flowers and trees delighted our eyes and the courtesy and beauty of the people were unforgettable. Bill was right. The trip was not without its funny moments too. Not long afterwards Bill gave up smoking, but I thought - as a treat - I would get him some cigars. As he smoked his face assumed an unusual expression.

'What's the flavour like?'

'Ah, mm-m, very interesting,' was his reply.

A local standing nearby began doubling up with laughter and pointed out, with great amusement, that he was smoking it from the wrong end! Enough to put you off smoking for life!

We spent many more fascinating days in Burma and returned reluctantly to Rangoon before flying to Calcutta to catch our flight home. We wanted to inspect the Rangoon zoo while we were there, although someone told us not to bother as 'most of the animals are dead'. We went all the same. It more or less lived up to our expectations, or lack of them. A few monkeys in a treeless, dusty, moat-encircled compound; a motionless crocodile in a twenty-foot murky pond. Bears begging and grimacing to attract your attention, hoping to be fed. Some Indian rhino standing forlornly in their pen. As we watched, feeling more and more depressed, a lanky chap came and greeted us with 'Hello, I'm Charlie the tiger master'. It turned out he was also the head of the zoo. He proudly showed us the tigers and lions, and elephants shackled by an eight-foot chain to a post, endlessly swaying. Charlie told us they were walked in the early mornings round the zoo and bathed. I wanted to believe him.

Charlie unburdened his heart to us and told us that in fifteen years he would leave Burma and join his brother in the Philippines. I wonder if he ever did. He also said it made him sad to see animals in cages. 'I know they cry', he said, 'they should be free'. We took him back to the hotel for a drink. If only all his dreams could come true.

Our final drive was to the British cemetery where we found the graves of over 2,000 Second World War soldiers. A quiet little oasis of memories, beautifully kept by the Commonwealth War Graves Commission. Most gravestones had a name engraved on them. Others simply read 'Soldier of the Second World War, Known unto God'.

The names of the Gurkhas who were killed were listed on the columns of the Memorial Building. Many of Bill's friends and in his regiment had lost their lives and he recognised countless comrades. It was traumatic.

'I don't like to read the names on the stones,' he said, 'in case I find my own there.'

I believe that part of him did die in the war. Certainly it was an experience of such a profound nature that life afterwards was, in a way, like a re-incarnation.

⌣

SEPTEMBER 28TH 2007. About 400 of us waited in the rain outside the Burmese Embassy in London. I'd decided the previous evening that I just had to go – for Bill and for my own memories of that beautiful country and its people. The emotional force of the monks' demonstrations which we had all been watching on television was proof – if it was needed – of the deep unhappiness and desperation within Burma. The agony of their repression and isolation and the worsening economic situation. The inability to give children adequate food and health care.

I was the fourth person to arrive, joining a little group of a nun and her two Burmese companions. 'Free Burma' was written on small pieces of cardboard. Gradually more people started to appear, with placards, photos of Aung San Suu Kyi, strips of red cloth which we were all given to wear. There was a handful of Europeans, mostly elderly or old like myself, but Burmese young and old filled the street. Suddenly we were told that monks were coming and a space was made on the pavement. One of them, deeply respected, began hitting a kind of drum and intoning prayers. Later, more monks arrived and everyone joined in chanting and singing. A young Burmese next to me explained that one of the songs had been sung during the uprising in 1988. Feelings were tangible.

The protest was peaceful, ordered but passionate. Watched – benignly I felt – by the police guarding the Embassy whose door bore a sign saying it was closed until 2.30 pm. When presumably the demonstration would be over. I wondered what those people tucked away behind the Embassy curtains were thinking. There were two men watching the crowd whose 'look' and demeanour were chilling. The first, a slight man in a dark coat, stood nearby the Embassy door and looked at us unflinchingly, like a predatory bird, sharp, penetrating. The other was a Burmese who, holding a small camera, walked up and down in front of the crowd, recording all the faces. Someone whispered to me that the images might be sent to Burma and, if any of those individuals could be identified, their families could be punished. I could well believe it.

Press and TV cameras milled about and one reporter with a microphone came up to me and asked why I was there. I explained about Bill and of my disgust at the way Burma's leaders treated the people who are helpless victims.

I don't know how this will end. A UN official is going to Burma today, the 29th, and I pray he will be allowed to see Aung San Suu Kyi. But, in the short term, I don't feel optimistic. What chance do unarmed helpless people have against men with guns? No different really from wild animals and armed hunters.

~

24 OCTOBER 2008. A crowd of us stood on the far side of Portland Place, facing the Chinese Embassy in London, in protest at China's support for the Burmese junta. We were herded behind a kind of mesh fence, where we stood holding our placards and banners. Police presence was fairly heavy. After a while someone asked for thirteen volunteers to hold up Aung San Suu Kyi masks in front of their faces

Virginia McKenna

and stand on the central pavement of the road with our backs to the Embassy. I joined the line. Pictures were taken. People stared from buses and cars.

When we returned to the others, a chant began – 'Free Burma – Free Burma – Free Aung San Suu Kyi – Now – Now.'

A huge replica key had been made with the names of over 2,000 people that are currently being held in Burma as political prisoners. The monks and one or two others then crossed to the Embassy door to request the acceptance of the key by the authority there. A few moments later they returned to our side of the road, still holding the key. I couldn't believe it. What does it take to touch men's hearts?

Thoughts at Home

THESE DAYS, FOR THE first time in my life, I am not sharing it with a dog, or two - or sometimes three. In 2006 I had to have our beautiful Sarda put to sleep. Without going into the whole story, we found her in Sardinia and one year, after Bill died, when I went out to our house on my own I found her sitting on the terrace. Her owner, who had rented our house for a while, no longer wanted her and had given her to the caretaker of the house next door. But she seemed to like being at ours! I asked the caretaker if he would be willing to give her to me so I could bring her to England. He was fine about it, as he already had three dogs to look after.

So, I made all the arrangements, and when my youngest son, Dan, drove out in his truck, he returned with Sarda as an extra passenger. She had a cheerful and accepting nature and didn't seem too bothered about the six months' quarantine. We visited her regularly and I had her groomed every so often so she had nice kind hands reassuring her. I already had my Bess, that my second son Justin and I

With Bess.

Virginia McKenna

rescued from the Battersea Dogs Home, and I wasn't quite sure how they would get on together. Bess was a very different temperament. Nervous, insecure and devoted to me, I didn't want her to feel usurped in any way. There were, I admit, some tricky times and a few quarrels. Both dogs were large and strong and sometimes it was a challenge to calm them down. But as the years passed, and Bess got older, they settled into quite a steady accepting relationship. Indeed, when I had to have Bess put to sleep, Sarda became very withdrawn and depressed for several weeks. We both missed her terribly.

We have shared our lives with many fascinating, lovable and faithful dogs. It was a miniature poodle, Ginny-puppy, that arrived in the early 1950s; later, we kept two of her puppies, Auntie Lou and Boy. Poor Lou suddenly went blind and never was able to cope with her darkened world. Most of the time I carried her around and then she was reassured. But her confidence left her, as did her interest in life.

Two RSPCA rescue dogs, of the Heinz variety, bounded into our garden later on. Bonaparte (who turned out to have a rather unpredictable nature) and Wellington, who was a gentle peacemaker. We adored them.

It was when we were in Kenya, filming *Born Free*, that we decided we just couldn't be without a dog. The children were desperate to have one, so one Sunday we answered an advertisement and drove up to Thomson Falls. There we met a fascinating lady, Violet Carnegie, and her cluster of Border Collie puppies. We came home with Nell. A month or two before filming ended we sent her to England, to begin her period of quarantine, and my father-in-law visited her regularly. What joy it was when the moment came to bring her home.

Beautiful little Katie was our next Border Collie, but she came to a sudden and untimely end. We had been walking in the woods with the dogs when, on arriving home, we realised she wasn't with us. Finally we found her. Dead. We took her to the vet and were told she had been bitten by a snake. There are adders here. We were heartbroken.

Then we got a trio. From a farm. Merlin (he was a Blue Merle), Shadow and Wolfie. Unfortunately, we had to rehome Merlin to a friend's friend, as the three dogs became a kind of 'pack' and frightened our neighbour. Shadow was the gentlest creature and truly lived up to his name. Wolfie was an enigma. He was feisty but quiet, a bit temperamental and hated being fussed over. We were always very careful when children were around. They both lived to a good age, but

Wolfie's end was strange. One day he went off down the field, although walking was a problem as he had arthritis, and by evening he hadn't returned. We searched everywhere. The next day we started again and I visited neighbours and others further afield, put up notices. All the things you do. We never saw him again. I just couldn't bear the thought of him dying alone. It was terrible. But then, as Will said, in nature animals do go off to die and we should respect that.

Writing about all these endearing dogs, it makes me long for another one!

There are some who have extreme views about animals. That even sharing your life with dogs and cats is unacceptable. I certainly would not condone keeping a bird in a cage, or a wild animal, or a rabbit in one of those small hutches you see in pet shops. (I know from watching the rabbits in my field how they love to gambol and play). But dogs and cats that have shared man's life for centuries? That, for me, is a step too far. To build up a natural relationship of respect and affection with an animal enhances life for both of you. And if I welcome another dog into my home, it will certainly be a 'rescue'.

Now I'm in a kind of limbo. There are ponies belonging to a friend grazing the field in front of the house, and I have a 'tame' pheasant, (Mr Fizzy) who comes for breakfast and tea to the kitchen door each day, but I just can't - yet - take on a new responsibility.

IT IS grey today. I hear the sound of a leaf-blower machine. We are starting to prepare the tubs and containers for the bulbs. A few geraniums valiantly blaze their reds and pinks, but soon they will carefully be lifted and put in the little greenhouse for the winter. I've started to fill the birdfeeder and small fluttering bodies gratefully crowd round as I watch through the window.

Some people find autumn sad and depressing. I love it. The changing colours, the energy going back deep into the soil, mysteries of growing and living out of sight but there, nevertheless. And, of course, the view from my window ever changes, the trees' shapes are revealed, unclothed. The field. Grey-green. Quiet.

Virginia McKenna

What colour is the field?
Corn gold, snow white, grass green, earth brown?
No matter.
It is the womb, the grave,
The larder of both wild and human beasts.
It is your quiet space
From which your thoughts can seek their path
To heaven.

Sit silent in the field.
Open your mind and heart.
Wait for the sign.
The butterfly that lights upon your hand.
The leaf that falls from one far-distant tree.
The poignant music from the blackbird's throat.
Be still.
He will be there.

Who is 'he'? When I wrote this poem I was thinking of Bill. I hope always for a 'sign' that he is with me, and often he is. I do believe, very strongly, that the spirit never dies. Indeed on two or three occasions I have experienced a physical confirmation of this and it is comforting. However strong we try to be, we all need comforting sometimes.

I'm trying to come to terms with a new, indisputable realisation that quite soon - who knows how soon - I too may be that butterfly alighting on one of my children's hands. Even when you are in your middle years you don't really stop to think much about the final ones. But now this thought is never far from me. Possibly the life I lead is hastening that moment - travelling, always busy, finding it hard to say no to anything connected to our work at Born Free. I know I stop and look at the view and the trees and the plants in my garden more than I used to. I feel inordinately happy when one of my children phones or comes round and when I see my grandchildren. I store all these precious moments away in my heart with a new intensity and revisit them when I feel a bit sad. Because they bring you back to life these young people - with all their talents and idiosyncrasies and fun and sweetness.

Sometimes it's hard to stand back when one or other of them is struggling with personal problems. But I believe they know I am there for them. At any time. While I still can be.

Normandy

MY MOTHER'S MOTHER, ANNABELLA, or GrinGran as I called her, was always there for me. A constant factor in a somewhat higgledy-piggledy childhood. My grandfather, Etienne, died young. He was 'in cotton' in Le Havre in Normandy and was comfortably off. He and GrinGran and their four children – my mother, my aunt Marguerite (Maggie), and my uncles Peter and John, lived in a tall imposing house high on the hillside overlooking the famous *falaises* (cliffs) at Etretat on the Normandy coast. However, when he died the family fortunes changed dramatically. Unfortunate handling of the family money eventually led to my grandmother leaving Les Charmettes to move to a little two-bedroomed gardener's cottage even further up the hill. It must have been traumatic for them all.

Although I know I stayed in the big house (as I have photos of myself and my cousin Johnny taken in the garden), my memories reside in the little ivy-clad cottage with its lavender-bordered path. Here I had countless summers with my darling grandmother. She had a cook-housekeeper who lived in, so GrinGran and I shared a bedroom and lay chattering away about this and that when we turned out the light. She was my special friend in whom I could confide my heartaches and teenage confusions. I knew she would never be judgmental but listen and nod and offer sound, practical suggestions – if they were needed. She let me have watered-down wine at lunchtime, and then I would walk in the woods above the cottage looking for wild strawberries.

My Uncle Peter was often there in the summer. He was a pianist, a teacher – and a loner. He never married and lived the most frugal of lives in his tiny flat in Paris. Later on, Bill and I used to worry about him and always brought him to our home at Christmas – and again in the summer. We became 'his' family. Louise adored him. They spent hours playing duets on the piano and we still shed tears when we remember him – his thick glasses and his beret and his courteous, old-fashioned manner. We were completely taken aback when, on his death, we discovered he, in fact, had quite a considerable amount of

Virginia McKenna

money. He spent nothing on himself as he wished to leave it to his nephew and niece and their children. I found that quite heartbreaking but, in a way, completely in character.

In Etretat he gave me French lessons, sitting on the old green bench near the tennis court. 'You were quite a strict professor!' I told him once. He was amazed and quite upset in case he had been unkind to me.

During the war he joined the infantry and Uncle John the French Cavalry. My aunt lived in Paris (she was Directrice of Molyneux, the famous fashion house), while my grandmother stayed in Normandy. In South Africa my mother waited anxiously for news but it came rarely and letters were censored. One incident we learned about later was alarming, to say the least. Uncle Peter was visiting Etretat and had gone for a walk on the cliff. He saw a farmer and casually enquired if there were any Germans around. The farmer decided he was a spy and reported him to the German headquarters in the town. Whereupon my uncle was arrested and driven to Rouen and put in prison! When my grandmother found out she marched down the hill to the headquarters and demanded to see the Commandant. He was quite taken aback, and agreed to drive her himself to Rouen with a change of clothes for Uncle Peter that GrinGran insisted he must have! In the end all was well and the traumatic events ended with Uncle Peter returning with them to Etretat. My grandmother was a brave and wonderful lady.

Eventually she was unable to live on her own any longer and it was decided to bring her to England to live with my mother and her husband Charles Oakeley. He had a large house in Frittenden in Kent. I went to fetch her from France. Not an easy experience to leave your whole adult life behind and 'start again'. No more to see the white cliffs arching on the skyline and the sea shimmering beyond. No more visits to the market and the bread shop, the exchange of news with friends, the slow, ever more laborious climb up the hill to the cottage. My grandmother never complained or showed a sense of loss, but I'm sure it was there.

She lived just long enough to see my daughter Louise as a baby in 1960 and I have a greatly loved photo of the four generations. Louise's second name is Annabella. We must keep alive the names of those we love. And treasure the things that belonged to them.

When my mother died, I inherited GrinGran's desk and a wall cabinet and an impressive Russian copper 'urn'. It has a basin beneath and a tap shaped like a fish. You can fill the copper 'urn' with water and then wash your hands in the basin. I also have her beautiful pearl drop earrings which she wore often. All these 'objets' have special meaning for me, but none more so than a little pale blue scarf with dots that she loved. A keepsake I keep safe.

It is these little things that matter most, isn't it? During the first spring Bill and I spent together, he said it was tradition to give lily of the valley on the first of May. A small cotton handkerchief adorned with these flowers lies near the little spotted blue one.

I loved Les Charmettes. The house stood empty and echoing after the war, but in my mind the rooms resounded with family voices and the energies of my grandparents, my mother, my aunt and uncles. In their time the house was filled with music - piano, cello, singing - I remember my mother telling me how the children sat on the stairs to listen to the playing of French pianist Robert Casadesus, who was a friend of my grandfather.

But the war had left its legacy. Etretat had been occupied by the Germans and subsequently by the Americans. Each had left their crude graffiti, defacing this charming old home. GrinGran and I

Above: GrinGran's garden staircase in Normandy.

Top right: The decaying greenhouse in GrinGran's garden.

Right: With my cousins Etienne and Johnny at Les Charmettes.

Below: Four generations – my mother, GrinGran, baby Louise and me, with Bill, his daughter Anna and Will.

were outraged and we marched down from the cottage, armed with buckets and soap and brushes, and scrubbed the ugly words off the flaking walls.

It is heartening to know that the house was eventually bought by a family who loved it too – and in 2001 I went with my son Dan and his partner Adnana to revisit Etretat, which had played such an important part in my younger life. To Dan, family matters hugely and he had often asked if we could go there to walk on the pebbled beach, visit the patisserie and try and take a peek into the cottage garden, up on the hill. I resisted the temptation for a long time. For me, Etretat without GrinGran meant little and I knew it would be an emotional journey. But, in the end, I felt touched that Dan wanted to go and so we went on Eurostar with the car and drove along the Normandy coast, marvelling at the beautiful old houses and little villages, largely unchanged – the wide, flat landscapes with fields as far as the eye could see and the pale, winter sky vast and limitless. The New Year was almost upon us, and it seemed such a personal and heartwarming way to touch a moment of the past before welcoming in the future.

We did walk on the beach, and past the casino where my fourteen-year-old mother had scandalised the community by dancing the Charleston in a concert! We went into the patisserie, had coffee and palmiers, and Dan delighted in the murals on the wall, painted by Raphael Cramoysan, the son of GrinGran's gardener.

But then we ventured up the hill to the big house, tried the handle on the little ancient door which led up damp, cold steps into the lower part of the cottage garden, and went in. We felt like thieves, stealing into someone else's privacy. It was a place which still – in a very poignant way – belonged to me. The steps, the smell of mildew, the old greenhouse, now in decay. The dahlia beds, once the pride of Cramoysan. The tennis court, and the summerhouse, where GrinGran dried the lavender on huge china plates, were gone. Instead, another house had been built. It was strange and new and had no meaning. The cottage was different too. Another room had been added and the buzzing lavender bushes that lined the path had disappeared. Still, it was where I had spent most of my childhood summers, and beyond. How could I help my tears?

We walked back down to the steps and then saw a group of people coming up the sloping path from Les Charmettes. We had been discovered! Never mind, the present owners of the big house were delightful. I explained who we were and about my grandmother ('Ah – Madame Dennis!') and they invited us down to the house for coffee. It was quite overwhelming. Raphael Renard is an architect. His father had bought the house and now Raphael, Virginie (!) and their four children lived there. A family home once more. Though, sadly, the family has now broken up and Raphael lives there on his own.

We went back to Etretat later – this time with Louise and her eldest son Lindon. Raphael and the children came over to England to visit us. Now and again he sends me beautiful images of the famous falaises and the chapel on the hill. The deep, damp smell of the old steps and the shape of the little cottage overwhelm me. I remember canoeing through the 'portes' in the cliffs with my cousin Johnny and a crowd of friends and picnicking on another pebbled beach further down the coast. Dancing to a gramophone in someone's house, being late for lunch and arriving breathless in GrinGran's little room and trembling under the stare of disapproval from Suzanne, her cook. Nothing that a glass of watered wine didn't mend!

Dan would like to go again. Perhaps I will, just once more. For him.

Zoo Campaigns

I FEEL DRAWN IN A million different directions. Deep down all I want is to be still. At home. Seeing my family. Playing with my grandchildren. Pottering in the garden. But other emotional strings are pulling towards my family in Australia, to be part of an animal campaign, to travel to do a 'Zoo Check' or attend a conference. My Born Free life. It is impossible to turn my back on all that Bill and I agonised over. How can I betray all those creatures in captivity whose eyes haunt me to this day. Some, by now, dead and gone. Others, tragically, still victims of man's manipulation and lack of real understanding of what a wild animal is.

Bill and I travelled to endless countries and visited countless zoos in Europe, India, the USA. Over and over again the story repeats itself. The only thing that changes is the language on the cage signs. After Bill died I carried on whenever I could, and added China to the list of nightmare experiences. Last year it was China again, after a week spent in Thailand.

Over the past three years, three zoos I've visited have become personal challenges. It was Bill who first visited the zoo in Limassol, Cyprus, in 1991. We had had countless letters from visitors to the zoo, tourists who could not tolerate the sight of baboons, bears, lions, leopards and an elephant (now long dead) enduring their pitiful, cramped conditions. Bill decided to take a look – his film footage was shocking. We wrote letters, we visited again and met some of those in charge. Bill went back again with a friend of ours, Gervase Farjeon, in 1993. A fateful trip. Bill and Gervase both caught pneumonia and had to go to hospital. It was an illness from which Bill never regained his full strength, and I feel it precipitated his death in March 1994. He worked till the end.

I took up this baton and went out with the BBC for their programme *State of the Ark* and then later with our vet, John Knight. We contacted the World Society for the Protection of Animals (WPSA) who had said they would re-home the zoo's two bears – something they have now achieved.

Virginia McKenna

Top: A bear and an orang-utan in Pata Store Zoo, Bangkok.

Above: With BFF vet John Knight and HSH Prince Albert of Monaco, preparing Pitou the leopard for her journey.

Right: Pitou released from her travelling crate.

Below: Pitou and Sirius in the Julie Ward Education and Rescue Centre at Shamwari, South Africa.

Suddenly, unbelievably, as we enter the final weeks of 2008, it appears we have the 'green light' to re-home the three leopards from the zoo. Never give up!

In the early nineteenth century there was an animal menagerie, the Exeter Exchange, in a commercial building in Central London. In 2007 there is an animal menagerie in a store on the outskirts of Bangkok. Thailand, Pata Store Zoo. In May 2006 I am ascending in a glass-sided lift to the top floor of a department store. As we rise I see the counters of bright clothes and furnishings, people browsing and shopping. The lift stops and we step into another world. The sound of animals, the smell of animals. Hardly a human in sight. We buy our tickets and enter a little hell. Chimpanzees, orang-utans, tigers, sunbears, black bears, monkeys, goats, deer, binturong, a gorilla, lemurs and two ponies. One so lame it could hardly move on its tiny patch of urine-splattered concrete. It stared at me and its eye burned into my brain. I don't know why but that was the look that turned me inside out. That eye. That desperate, pleading eye. I can't rest until I have done something to help these creatures. The bear standing on its hind legs frantically beating time to some raucous canned music pounding its noise into your brain. I'm planning for October...yes, that is my plan.

And now the Jardin Animalier in Monaco. After many years of unsuccessfully trying to persuade decision makers to allow us to suggest changes, to phase out this little collection, something exciting has started to happen. In August, after some exchanges of letters and a personal endorsement of our work from Anthony Osmond Evans, who was writing a coffee-table book about Monaco and HSH Prince Albert, I received an invitation to go to lunch with the Prince in Monaco. I was accompanied by Born Free's PR Director, Shirley Galligan, and we had a most encouraging meeting with him, beginning with a walk together round the Jardin during which he asked me if I could find a home for his two leopards. The hope I felt at that moment! Memories flooded back of the lion whose solitary roars desolately echoed back to him across the yacht-filled harbour below; Nina, the beautiful white tiger (who, I discovered, died from cancer a few months before) pacing her cage, her repetitive turning leaving its tell-tale brown smudge on the wall; the chimps and orang-utans; the black leopard with a tail wound; the rhino – all these animals were gone, relocated or dead. But, suddenly, there was the glimmer

Virginia McKenna

of something different – a new future. The Prince, a man of vision, with different values and a different outlook was in charge. I wanted to shout for joy but, in answer to his question about his leopards, I just replied 'I think I can offer you a home'.

So, on January 7th 2008, the leopards, Pitou and Sirius, began their long journey to South Africa, to a three-acre bush enclosure at our Julie Ward Education and Rescue Centre at Shamwari, near Port Elizabeth. The Prince came to say goodbye to them – participating, in the most visible way, in the final checks that our vet, John Knight, had to carry out after they were sedated. It was extremely touching and I felt a great weight lifted from me as I sensed the first really important steps were being taken to phase out this little menagerie. Like the leopards, most of the large animals had been taken in from circuses but, although well fed and looked after, the environment was wholly inappropriate. Even as I write Pitou and Sirius are happily settling in, eating well and exploring their new home with its myriad strange sounds and smells. From a circus trailer and a concrete zoo cage to a bush enclosure is a big leap. And this is only the beginning. They are the trailblazers.

I remember George Adamson's reply to a question I asked him once: 'Is there anything you regret having done during your time with Elsa?'

'Yes,' he said, 'sending her sisters to a zoo.'

How happy he would have been to see Pitou and Sirius under the African sun.

Murder at Kora

2008

I T IS NOW FEBRUARY, and I am coming to the end of my yearly visit to see Louise and her children in Australia. It has been a very hot day. It is almost six in the evening and the sun still burns. A parakeet flies high above me. Emerald against the evening blue. Its song, Vivaldi-themed, piercing the soft-wire drumming of the windblown leaves. One of the cats lazes by my knees. I think of Kenya. Of George. Of sitting with him and Bill in Kora in the warm night under the vast, star-crammed sky. The lions lying outside the camp fence. Hamisi, the cook, gone to a well-deserved rest after cooking a delicious supper over the little wood ash fire. George puffing his pipe and he, Bill and I having beer. We talk a little, soaking up the comfortable silence that can only exist between real friends. The Koh-i-noor diamond is nothing compared with the jewels in the sky above us – and you can never buy moments like this.

Some years before, in the late 1970s, we had taken the children on a camping safari to Kenya. The highlight was Christmas at George's camp. We have very dear and longstanding friends in Nairobi whom we first met when we made *Born Free*. Monty and Hilary Ruben and their brilliant daughters, Lissa and Mandy, have continued to offer us a home-from-home over the years. With his company, Express Transport, Monty Ruben expertly facilitated all the practical requirements needed by a film company on location and, indeed, continued to do so for most of the major feature films shot in Kenya. Including *Out of Africa*.

For our safari Monty had kindly lent us a Range Rover, which Bill drove, and I drove the hired VW camper van, equipped with tiny fridge and cooker.

George was loved deeply by all of us. People have often asked me 'What was his secret?' For he truly seemed to hold the key to real contentment and fulfilment. Hard to speak for someone else, but I believe that part of his 'secret' was his integrity. He was a whole man. In the latter years he lived the life he believed in. He was selfless and

Virginia McKenna

totally non-judgmental. A rare being. From all over the world people of all ages, all backgrounds were drawn to him. His simple camp, devoid of any semblance of the safari luxury we now see, was a place of true riches. Walking or driving with him through the bush, learning how to read the signs left by the animals that had passed down that same track, identifying the trees (I remember he showed me the frankincense tree and the three wise men came to life), walking along the bank of the Tana River and seeing a small pool in the sand containing baby crocodiles. ('The crocodile is the only animal that will bite you while it's still in the egg!' George chuckled.) And then there were 'his' lions.

At that time a young English boy, Tony Fitzjohn (still a friend of ours, but now Field Director of the George Adamson Wildlife Preservation Trust in Mkomazi, Tanzania, and an OBE), was working as George's assistant. George certainly needed one as he was rehabilitating a considerable number of lions and he was already in his mid-sixties. Tony was charismatic, capable and very much his own man. Our children thought he was wonderful, a kind of hero.

It was an unforgettable Christmas. The weaver birds bustled about around their nests, the ground squirrels foraged near the mess hut or jumped up on George's knee for a nut, the lions lazed outside the camp fence and we tucked into Christmas fare which we had brought with us from Nairobi. Hamisi taught me how to cook mince pies in

Top: George Adamson with 'his' lions at Kora – his man-made pride.

Above right: Christmas at Kora, 1974 – voted the best holiday ever! George, myself, Dan, Tony Fitzjohn, Louise, Justin, Will.

Below right: Our camper van on the way to George's camp, stuck in the sand!

Bottom left: 'The Nightingale', in which George was killed.

Bottom right: With Will at Elsa's grave, Meru.

Virginia McKenna

the hot ashes of his fire and we all helped with the washing up. Reluctantly we had to leave George, Hamisi and the lions, but they never left our thoughts.

Voted the best family holiday ever it was, in a way, like *Swallows and Amazons* in Africa. We camped anywhere, rose at dawn, slept at dusk, washed clothes when we found water and experienced an amazing freedom almost impossible to find now. We drove up into the Chyulu Range, the children running through the rainbow butterflies that fluttered and shimmered around us. We drove through the little rain-forest, its deep shadows and damp smell evoking strange imaginings. Out in the sun again we came across a boy, not more than seven or eight years old, herding the family livestock. Skills and responsibilities the children in the Western world know nothing of at that age or beyond. That sweet friendly wave from the boy was Kenya for me. However ragged the clothes, dilapidated the home, however hard the struggle for survival, the generosity of spirit towards us, mere visitors, driving around in our vehicles with little real understanding of their way of life, always touched me deeply.

Our last night in Kenya. We camped in the Amboseli National Park campsite. No-one else was there. It was like our private piece of paradise. We sat quietly after supper, as the light faded and the night sounds began to emerge. A distant roar reminding us of earlier days. Time to sleep. Bill and Will disappeared into the little tent, and I settled down with the other three children, the back of the camper van open, but screened with a mosquito net.

Our 'family whistle' woke me. 'Lions outside,' Bill whispered. I peered through the window to see a huge pride of lions slowly walking by the camper, stumbling over the guy ropes of the tent, and finally coming to rest in the clearing. The moon shone its brilliant, cool light. We were all transfixed. The cubs played, the mothers stretched and yawned, the males exuded their majesty. They stayed several hours, and then an unseen signal changed the mood. As silently as they had arrived, they slowly disappeared into the darkness.

For us it was a never-to-be-forgotten farewell.

THE VERY last time Bill and I went to Kora it was different. 1989. George's life ended. Murdered, like Joy, by a man. Both he and Joy had lived with wild predators, taken risks and faced danger, but – in the end – humans dealt the final blow.

A plane had 'buzzed' the camp, signalling it was about to land on the little airstrip. Inge – a nurse from Germany, who was a friend and a regular visitor to the camp, went off to meet it with Bitacha (the cook, Hamisi's, assistant). George remained in camp at his old type-writer. The recorded accounts vary but whatever the truth of it was, the outcome was irrefutable. The bandits appeared from the bush, shoot-ing, demanding money. Bitacha's thigh was crushed with a crowbar, Inge was pulled into the bushes.

At camp the shots were heard. George and four of his men jumped into his old Land Rover, 'The Nightingale', and drove along the track. Ahead of him George saw the scene all too clearly. Two of his men sensed his intent and jumped out of the vehicle. George put his foot down and drove straight at the bandits. They shot him several times and, finally, in the back. George and two of his men were dead. Inge was safe. But 'The Nightingale' was silenced forever.

As Bill wrote, 'I think George was quite unaware of how much, in his quiet unassuming way, he had influenced people or how much he had given them. Hero to so many people while he lived, at 83 he died in one final flourish of bravery...and Ginny and I lost a very dear friend.'

Bill went on ahead to Kampi ya Simba (Camp of the Lions) and I flew up in a helicopter with Dr Richard Leakey, Director of the Kenya Wildlife Service (KWS), and some other Kenya Wildlife Service offi-cials. And the coffin. The aircraft air was heavy with the perfume of the floral tributes. Many friends had asked me to take flowers to the service and the roses and lilies and other exotic flowers from the Nairobi florist would be, I knew, unlikely visitors to the dry, arid thorn tree country of George's camp. I remember looking at the coffin, still unable to believe that, inside, was our dear, kind, funny and very special old friend. But then, of course, he wasn't. His spirit was amongst us, touching our hearts, unleashing the tortured animal cry from Hamisi as the coffin was lowered into the ground by the KWS Rangers. The 'Last Post' and 'Reveille' accompanied our tears and we trickled a handful of sand into the grave.

Two weeks later the pugmarks of several lions were seen around the burial place. He was remembered.

Virginia McKenna

I RETURNED to Kora with my son Will four years ago. It was rather like going back to Etretat when GrinGran had gone. The little huts had been restored. There were fewer trees. One of George's staff, now old himself, came to shake our hands and have a photo taken. The Kora 'tit', the famous high rocky hill not far from camp, was a familiar image from earlier days. I walked between the huts looking for something I knew I would never find. It was so quiet. So empty.

It would have been difficult to share those very poignant moments with anyone else but Will. Returning to George's camp and his grave opened deeply buried feelings, some of which had been born over 50 years ago. Immersed as Will is in the cause we champion and the work we do, with its unbroken umbilical cord linked to the past, its animals and the 'spirit of Elsa', as Joy used to say, he understood. It was like having Bill there. A comfort beyond words.

George lived at Kora for 19 years. He arrived in 1970, when Christian the lion came to his rightful homeland, and died when he was murdered in 1989. His legacy is incalculable. He did many extraordinary things in his life – some widely known and written about. But, as happens, even those can be forgotten. As I wandered around the camp I thought of our Christmas family visit, of the frankincense tree, laughter in the mess hut, the vulturine guinea fowl – never far from a free meal of nuts and seeds – of Terence, George's brother, 'dowsing' at the table in a search for a missing lion.

And George's man-made pride. At one time he had ten lions that he had found or been given, cubs that had been born. Of all sizes, ages and temperaments, George had united them, rehabilitated them, given them a chance.

By a strange coincidence one female, Arusha, had come from Blydorp Zoo in Rotterdam, where Elsa's sisters had been sent and from where Christian's father, Butch, had been moved to Ilfracombe Zoo in Devon. There is a mean justice somewhere in this.

George is buried next to his brother Terence and near his favourite lion of all, Boy. Boy, our old friend from *Born Free* days and George's adored companion, whom he had looked after through thick and thin, nursed when sick and, finally, had to shoot.

Human error often results in unimaginable tragedy. It was at the time when Christian was in Kora. One of George's assistants, Stanley, had gone against rules and walked outside the camp fence – to look for honey, it was thought. A terrible cry and a loud roar brought George and others running, to find Boy holding Stanley in his mouth. George yelled at Boy, who dropped Stanley and backed off. George shot Boy through the heart. Stanley never recovered from his wounds and, I guess, the pain of what he was forced to do never really left George.

I laid some dried flower sprays on each grave and felt I was doing it for Bill, my children and all those whose lives had been touched by this extraordinary, modest pioneer. There is something about one's body returning to the earth. Like the animals. George would have wanted it no other way. Nor would we.

Virginia McKenna

Zanskar, Land of Buddhism

I T ISN'T REALLY VERY far from the Kora 'tit' to the Shingo La Pass, in Zanskar, northern India. Not in my mind's eye anyway. Looking down from the dry African hilltop or from the soaring snow-covered pass in Zanskar my spirit was uplifted. And humbled. So much connected these two places. The simplicity, toughness and challenges of living, the generosity and warmth of the people, the reality of one's own place in nature. In one land surrounded by endless miles of dry thornbush, in the other by the towering, shimmering peaks of the Himalayas.

In 1987 I took part in a Channel 4 series, *The World at Your Feet*. Coincidentally, I had just been asked to do a costume drama for the BBC. Without a second's hesitation I knew what I wanted to do. How could I resist the challenge and excitement of climbing ('no, it's not a climb', they said, 'it's a walk that could be done by any healthy, adventurous family') on the western Ladakh border.

The tiny Kingdom of Zanskar, surrounded by huge mountains, lies at the northern tip of India. To reach it one must scale passes of over 16,000 feet and travel between June and November. For seven months the valley and its inhabitants hibernate under a deep snow and ice mantle, awaiting the thaw and the brief time when planting, reaping and storing would consume all their time and energies.

For the trip there were so many things to do and to learn. Get the right walking boots, sun block, thermals, headache pills, tummy pills, light waterproof jacket. 'Climb high, sleep low' – this can avoid many physical problems, particularly headaches. Water bottle, small rucksack. And best of all, Bill came too. A check-up with his heart specialist assured us he would be fine to take on this 'walk'. That he was, in the face of the reality that eventually faced us, proved he really was in good shape, as was his unfailing determination not to be beaten by health concerns.

We flew to India at the end of June and on July lst, in a small 40-seater piston plane, flew over high, sharp-ridged mountains, below us the fertile Kulu Valley dotted with two-storey houses of brick and wood. Some with wooden posts supporting the upper floor leaving the area below as a shelter for animals. The airport at Kulu had opened only six years before to tourist traffic, bringing with it the usual mixed blessings. Cars and lorries hooted their way through the busy streets which were lined with traders and their stalls, selling everything from cloth to sweetmeats to pots and pans.

Our bus was taking us to Manali. We passed small groups of women and children sitting by huge piles of stones and rocks which they were smashing with hammer-like tools. Their shacks looked pitiful – patchwork dwellings which surely contained few of life's comforts. Manali itself was like a small frontier town in a prosperous apple-growing area. Although beggars revealed a sadder side of the picture.

Our trek leader was Kuku, an experienced guide, who turned out to be one of the real blessings of our journey. He came from Kashmir and when he was very small had seen at his school a book with a picture of a lioness on the cover. He told us he had not been able then to read or write, but kept returning to that book to look at the pictures. He nearly fell off his chair when he heard that we had made the film of that book, *Born Free*!

We did a little filming in Manali. But Bill and I had done our own exploring before the film unit arrived. Shoes off, we entered the Buddhist temple and inhaled its peace. We looked in wonder at the imprints of Buddha's feet on a large stone slab. Dark corners were lit by a few flickering candles and the floor patterned by a scattering of flower petals. These moments, and another when Bill and I went into the forest to sit where Nehru had come to meditate during his visit to Manali, were stored away to soothe us on the less peaceful days ahead.

Early on the Friday we walked up to Old Manali, a place frozen in time. Wooden houses, carved, arched windows without glass. Women spinning, carrying wood in conical-shaped panniers, sifting and sorting the grain for the winter store. Shy, giggling children... 'What is your good name?' they called. And 'what is *your* good name?' I laughed. It was all so innocent and wonderful.

But this bliss changed to disappointment when we climbed higher to a flat area of land to watch the rehearsal for a dance; the musicians blew their amazing six foot-long silver horns (used only on religious or very important occasions), the men danced in their bright clothes, some dressed as women. Suddenly, the Oracle of the village appeared. He had been performing a ceremony which culminated in a trance.

He was shouting and shaking violently from head to foot. An old woman on the other side of the group started shouting back. The tension rose and when it stopped several people came to the Oracle and massaged him to restore his circulation. At first we didn't know what to do, but it was explained that the Oracle had said the musicians and dancers shouldn't perform for us. If they did the sky would fall down and kill everyone. We left, of course.

We were a very mixed, 'ad hoc' group of people on the trek. Kuku, our guide, Naresh Sohal, the Indian composer and his partner Janet, Michael Green, our wildlife adviser and wild flower identifier, Michael Seymour (doing his first film as a director), Dilshad the continuity girl, Shenni the production manager, Dr Gupta – and, of course, the muleteers, the cook and other members of the small film crew. Bill and I were the oldest in the party.

The organisation and planning of the trek left a lot to be desired. But we all coped in our different ways, though there were many opportunities lost, amazing situations not filmed. It was exhausting, frustrating and bewildering. But nothing and no-one could destroy the actual experience of walking and climbing in a pristine wilderness. The wild flowers, the images of mountains, valleys, *chortens* (sacred stone mounds), *mani* walls (with religious inscriptions), prayer flags, rosy-cheeked children, turquoise-studded head-dresses of the women. These are what I remember. Funny moments too.

Lying fully dressed in our sleeping bags after supper listening to the Men's Finals at Wimbledon on Bill's transistor. In a state of very early morning doziness brushing my teeth with antiseptic footbalm instead of toothpaste! Biting on a piece of toast and losing a piece of tooth – luckily not a front one – which I hastily patched up with a piece of gutta percha that Bill found in his sponge bag. Waking up at about 15,000 feet before the final climb to the pass, with a very strange feeling in my eyes. I nudged Bill. 'Well, they do look a bit strange', he said, 'in fact I can hardly see them!' The altitude again – and Michael Green said my eyes would stay swollen like that until we went down. He was right. It was dark glasses for four days.

So many incidents, experiences, difficulties, small victories, as when we completed a seven hour walk, or washed our socks more than every three days. I could go on for a long time – it is almost a book in itself! Certain things stick in the memory. Our last trek to the Shingo La Pass was delayed for a day. We camped on a bare, windy

This page

Above: The trek in Zanskar.

Right: A 'knitting circle' with the ladies.

Below: The wedding party, with the bride in white.

Opposite page

Top: Last climb to Shingo La Pass.

Bottom left: The steps to Phuktal monastery.

Bottom right: Laundry time!

Virginia McKenna

mountainside – grey and stony with fast-moving icy streams on all sides. The air was very thin and we were quite breathless. Bed early and at 2 am Kuku came to tell us the trekkers ahead of us had experienced problems. They had walked too fast, become separated from their mules, and because the ground of the snow bridges was too soft the mules came back, leaving the people without tents, sleeping bags or food. So an unplanned rest day! We washed clothes, listened to the call of the snowcock and saw Brandt's mountain finch and black redstart. And one tiny, solitary white flower with a yellow-green centre, perhaps a member of the mustard family. My heart went out to this flower. Survival for everything up here is such an achievement. The colour of the flower, the deep crimson robe of the monk we saw coming down the mountain towards us, such simple things that take on huge significance. The monk was on a three day walk to borrow a book from another monastery! We talked to him on film and gave him a warm welcome and some food.

I went to watch the muleteers as they tended their animals, checked their hooves, made sure they had no sores or chafing. If I am honest, I never felt really comfortable about the use of these stoic, uncomplaining creatures as they picked their way across icy streams, manoeuvred round rocks and navigated steep mountainsides. They carried all our equipment and food and I knew there was a long way to go before they would reach a warm shelter and their backs were freed from their loads. I know they were trained for this, and that they were well looked after by their owners, but I suppose it was just another example of what we expect from animals. Bill and I certainly didn't take them for granted.

The moment to regroup has arrived. Up at 2.30 am, a nearly full moon, tea and porridge. We left at 3.30 am, torches firmly grasped. Kuku first, then me, then Bill. A slow, zigzag climb, very cold, uneven ground, staggeringly beautiful. After five hours we were exhausted. The Pass, at last – 16,800 feet. 8.10 am. Curiously, although some of the climb was filmed, our arrival wasn't. Bill took photos of us at the top, and of me placing a white stone on the wall of the shrine, a prayer for a safe continuation of our journey. The prayer flags cheerily fluttered, the mules began their slow descent.

We waited a while longer and then, as we began to follow them, we saw what could have been the most amazing shot. Far down, a tiny dark line, were the mules, the only things that seemed to move in this vast white shimmering panorama. The silence hummed. We were now in Zanskar, land of Buddhism.

There was a different atmosphere in Zanskar. It was a self-contained world. It felt intensely spiritual. *Chortens* - shrines - gleamed here and there and, as we descended into the green valley, I saw my first wild mammal, a marmot. What a thrill. And at the far end of the valley we can see the Monastery mountain, Phuktal, our goal. How close it looks! How far it really is!

It is so very beautiful here. What do I mean by that? It was not just the wild flowers, the colours and shapes of the mountains, the *mani* walls, the carvings of Buddha. It was something to do with the intensity of the light, the purity of the landscape, nature uncluttered by man's inventions and structures and technology. Bill always used to say that true happiness is in working to survive. And that was the essence of Zanskar for me. That was what life was about, but embracing and uplifting the toughness of that struggle for survival was the spiritual belief that was interwoven with everyday life. Humbling and inspiring all at once. And, yes. Beautiful.

We had been walking for three hours when we heard extraordinary musical sounds and, over to our right, across a field, crowds of people and some tethered horses. Irresistible! Together with Michael Green and a couple of others we found ourselves in the middle of a wedding party! Most of the men were high on *chhang*, the local beer brew.

Seven men from the groom's family, wearing stunning gold hats, moved amongst the crowd. The bride herself, adorned in a collection of white cloths, was enacting a kind of play, crying and wailing, to show her reluctance to leave her family village. The 'band' played on, while women in headdresses bejewelled with turquoises, their hair puffed out with black wool, bent over some boxes, inspecting the dowry.

Initially we attracted curious stares, but it all turned out to be friendly. One rather merry middle-aged man offered his sister to Manoj, one of our guides, and said he would take me in exchange! I thanked him but felt I was a bit past it, as I had four children and a grandchild! Laughter all round.

Finally the bride was borne away by the seven splendid golden-hatted men and we set off again on our walk. About half an hour later, as we followed a very narrow mountain track by a river, we heard the sound of bells and horses' hooves. Cantering towards us was a procession taking the bride, who clung to the waist of the lead rider, to her husband's village. We hastily got off the path and watched the little white bundle of a bride, and her 'handmaidens' with their rosy cheeks and long black braids, disappearing into the distance towards a new life.

We reached the village of Testa. By now we were even more exhausted. Every bone ached. I longed to reach Phuktal and have some moments to reflect, be quiet, distance myself – even for a short time – from the physical demands and difficulties of the trek and the film schedule. But the Monastery was still five hours away.

We set up camp at Testa and I washed grain with the singing women and laughed with the gorgeous children – children are the best medicine of all.

We left at 6 am the next morning, following the Zanskar river up hill and down dale. Suddenly we saw a twig bridge crossing the water. Here and there slabs of stone were placed to tread on, and there was a low-slung rope of steel each side to hold on as we gingerly wobbled our way to the other side. Wild roses greeted us as we turned the corner and there, ahead of us, nestling in the high, precipitous cliffs like some strange, vast, fairytale palace was the Monastery. We entered another world.

We climbed steep steps carved from rock, and wound our way along narrow stone passages, watched by crimson-clad monks of all ages.

Eventually we reached a wide outer terrace from where we could look down over the valley far below. Ravens swooped and cawed around the Temple which was built above us in the cliff, its colourful decorations standing out vividly against the greyness of the rocky face.

Mats were brought for us to sit on and we were hospitably given tea and rice and curried dhal. Although, in return, we made a donation to the Monastery, I felt a pang of conscience knowing that every ounce of food must be carried up the long steep track.

The Lama joined us on the terrace and he and Naresh had a lively conversation, watched by the little boy monks. I remember looking round to see if this was being filmed, but no. Instead a meeting was set up in the Lama's room with him, Naresh and me sitting in a row on the floor. Not quite the same atmosphere! We stayed just a few hours and then bade our goodbyes.

I imagined life here during the winter months, life based on self-denial, meditation, abandonment of material possessions. How trivial seemed our grumblings and how selfish our concern for our own comforts!

Our trek was soon to end. Goodbye to the rosy-cheeked boys herding the yaks on the high pastures, to the Gaddi shepherds (said to be descendants of deserters from Alexander the Great's army) with their vast flocks of sheep, to the mules and their muleteers – the true heroes of this journey – who would repeat the trek many times until summer ended. Then the valleys would be covered with snow and the passes closed. The people will have stored their grain, their animal feed and their dried yak dung for fuel. The little communities will be isolated from each other until the snows melt, the birds build their nests and colour returns to the landscape.

The trek was over, but a surprise awaited us. Our producer must have heard how exhausted we all were and invited us to stay for a night on a houseboat. Srinagar, capital of Kashmir. Bill knew it from the war and knew how this brief moment of calm would soothe our aches and rest our minds.

We were still covered in dust and grime, our dirty clothes stuffed into bags and we must have looked a sorry sight! But after a shower, exchanging boots for sandals and putting on clean clothes, we both sank into the pleasure of gazing out over the lake, the peace, the stillness, the cool drinks and delicious food.

The next day we watched the small boats on the lake with their cargoes of flowers or fruit, crafts or jewellery. Bill gave me some beautiful earrings. Rani, our producer, most generously gave me a ring with a turquoise. It was all somewhat unreal I have to say. We walked round the town for a while and I sensed how at home Bill felt. I honestly believe many of his deepest feelings are buried in India.

I AM overwhelmed. I have just found a secret gift. Handwritten pages by Bill, written for me, and about me, in January 1988. After our Zanskar trek. I am awash. Words I have never read before:

Ireland is where my forefathers came from
And I am part of its history.
The McKennas
Once King makers
Scratched their names on its stones...
And fell asleep in its dust.

I've always wanted
To walk on Ireland's bright green earth
Along its velvet valleys
Watch heavy clouds on lazy golden streams
And feel the fresh breath of mountains
On my cheeks...in my lungs.

But I am Gemini
And as I walk at dawn
Wet-eyed in the eyeless morning,
My thoughts race ahead
Across the shadowless sleeping hills
Towards the smoking white peaks
Of the Himalayas...and I am there.

The trees are gone...save one or two
...and rice fields favour streams
Precious life from blocked-up veins
In squares of Ireland's green.

At the end of the valley
On ten inches of track
Five hundred feet above the ice-bridged stream –
Plunging and rearing
Bucking like a white
Fear-crazed stallion, I see
Red roses, pinks and clematis.
And further on a bridge of sorts
Stones laid across ropes
... swaying...swaying...

Virginia McKenna

Daring you to approach the monastery
The Phuktal – bricked-up in the cracks
Of an over-hanging cliff... I go...
Will Buddha sit on my head
If I move silently
In the shadows of the cross?

It is raining outside, my stove crackles warmly and above it, on the wall, is my collection of some of the wild flowers I gathered and pressed on our journey. The colours haven't faded, and I still have my climbing boots.

Today it is fourteen years since Bill died. He is still with me in spirit. Yes, I am with him at the shrine on top of Shingo La and the prayer flags beckon.

Sardinia

WHAT COULD BE FURTHER from a mountain top than the world beneath the sea? A secret world with its ever-changing patterns of light and and constantly moving fishes and plants. A world explored by our family since we built our holiday home in Sardinia over thirty-five years ago. When I first started writing this book the plan was to sell the house, but it is deeply loved by many of us and it was decided to try and keep it a little longer.

Bill found the pristine, uninhabited piece of land bordering the sea irresistible and we started to build the house of washed river stone around the fantastically shaped rocks on the coastline. From the sea the house is almost invisible but, with a few hops, skips and jumps, one can reach the beach from our terrace. Here all our children learned to swim and Bill started an informal diving 'school' which attracted lots of the other children who came to the beach. Indeed, one rock is called 'the diving rock'! That first summer, while the builders toiled, we camped in tents on the beach (no longer permitted). We made friends with an Italian family camping next to us, sampling the enviable culinary skills of Maria Teresa. I tried my best to return the hospitality, sweating over a tiny two-ring camping stove which produced less than cordon bleu results! In those days the shepherd led his sheep to graze on the nearby hill and our youngest son Dan used to visit him in his stone hut along the dirt road to sample 'sheep's cream'. Wild lavender grew in profusion, prickly pear created natural fence lines, a cormorant or two visited the bay, spreading their wings to dry as they perched on a rock.

We eventually bought an inflatable boat and an outboard motor and took ourselves off with towels, goggles and picnic to the islands of Cavoli and Serpentara. Crystal clear water revealed fragments of wreckage from old ships which the children dived to retrieve and, at Cavoli, a primitive statue of the Madonna and Child requires a ritual visit whenever we go. It touches one's heart to see this image resting silently on the sea floor. Once a year, in July, a flotilla of little boats goes out and the locals and holiday-makers scatter flowers on the water above these 'relics'.

Above: We camped on the beach watching our house being built.
Below: The view from the hillside overlooking our bay.

It was on the more distant island of Serpentara that, one year, Bill discovered an extraordinary plant. The pitcher plant. He was tremendously excited about it and contacted Sean Morris at Oxford Scientific Films. Sean came out to Sardinia and a second boat trip was taken to look at this extraordinary 'creation'. Not long after, a film on carnivorous plants was made. Captivatingly sinister, *Deathtrap* was a co-production between Oxford Scientific Films and Bill's company Morning Star.

Now, everything has changed. There are houses all around us. The village has grown into a small town with amazing shops and excellent restaurants. But sitting on the terrace at the end of the day, looking out to sea, the horizon remains dreamlike. The boats still make their way back to harbour from a day's fishing or fun. We still rinse out sand and salt from swimming costumes as grandchildren return from the beach for supper. *Plus ça change!*

Only yesterday
We hovered like fireflies
Over aquamarine cathedrals of light
And iridescent silver.

Only yesterday
We silently streaked
Through submarine grottos of deepest shade
And lightest light.

Shy visitors
Loosened from our feet of clay
Skimming like thistledown
On Neptune's liquid ceiling.

Seductive fingers
Of sea plants waved and beckoned
From secret moorings in the flickering sand
Elusive sirens forever songless.

And now today,
I close my eyes against the sun
I dream my dreams beneath the stars
And gaze forever at that magic world.

Ring of Bright Water

T HEY ARE NOT MY 'possessions', but they are the greatest treasures I have. My children and grandchildren and – great-grandchild. Our three sons live very near me. Between them they have five children.

Families! I don't know what I would do without my children – and theirs. From their birth to my old age they have filled my life with joy. Even the difficult and sometimes painful moments have been weathered, accepted, resolved. We all have our weaknesses, failings and idiosyncrasies whatever age we are. But blood is, indeed, thicker than water. In my heart I sometimes feel like an old lioness defending her young against outside forces. Almost all living creatures are compelled by instinct to live in families.

In 1968 we made a film based on Gavin Maxwell's memorable book *Ring of Bright Water*. A house was rented on Loch Etive, and relays of family and friends joined us during our three months on the West Coast of Scotland. Our darling Uncle Peter came from France and my

close friend and sister-in-law Alice and Clifford her husband, drove up from London, to the delight of the children.

There was a rowing boat on the shore and one day I took Uncle Peter out on the loch to see the seals. As we neared the rock where they were lying in the sun, I noticed an extremely large black shape between us and the shore. 'Look round behind you very carefully, Uncle Peter' I said, 'I think there is a basking shark between us and the shore'.

'Where, where?' Uncle Peter exclaimed, leaping instantly to his feet so that the boat nearly toppled over! The wobbling of the boat and the startled seals splashing into the water from the rock suddenly changed the tranquil scene into one of confusion! The basking shark glided quietly on and calm was restored.

It was here that we made a new friend who, when filming ended, eventually came home with us to Surrey. Jonnie, the springer spaniel, had been hired to be 'my' dog in the film. He was a gun dog, a kennel dog, and had never belonged to a family before. He was very obedient and did all he was required to do in the film. But, somehow, there was no light in his eye. 'Can he come and live with us?' I said.

At first (for one night only as it transpired) Jonnie slept in the warm pantry by the kitchen. Slept is a misnomer. Howled is more like it! One night without any sleep was enough and we brought his basket into the bathroom which led off our bedroom. Peace was instantaneous! We had become his family!

But Jonnie was not only an 'actor' in the film. He also became a surrogate parent. One day the gardener of the property arrived at the house with a fawn in his arms. Abandoned, he said. Bottle feeding commenced and Bambi (of course) also became part of the family in a very short space of time. Jonnie was his favourite. In the evening he would potter about the sitting room, eventually curling up snugly next to Jonnie on the rug near the fire. Jonnie was tender and gentle with him and it was very touching to watch these unlikely friends enjoying each other's company. It was hard to part with Bambi when we left Loch Etive, but we found a forester in Staffordshire who had a fenced-off sanctuary area in the forests in Cannock Chase. So Bambi went there. (The first of two roe deer we raised as it turned out.)

We applied the same method of getting to know the otter who was to play 'Mij' in the film as we had with the lions during *Born Free*. Bill and I sat in a large hillside enclosure with a stream running below and the otter ('Mij') splashed in the water and scampered around the bushes, avoiding the two strange figures sitting higher up by some stones – ostensibly reading books. The breakthrough came five or six days later. Mij suddenly approached us and cautiously sniffed our boots. As the days passed the trust deepened and we played and had fun together. We were now friends.

When you try and recall work you did long ago, it is inevitable that what you most remember are the people, the atmosphere and, for me, the animals. The films I made when I had a 'real' career were in the 1950s and 1960s. In a way they can be divided into two parts, the war films in the '50s and the animal films in the '60s.

In *Ring of Bright Water* my character was not based on any identifiable individual. In a way it was a bit of 'poetic licence', someone to provide a human dimension within the main body of the story which was obviously focusing on the otters. For 'Dr Mary' I had to assume a Western Isles accent, and a very delightful lady came to our house and gave me a few lessons. It wasn't a very large part and really, for me, it was a joyful time. The beauty of the West Coast, working closely with Jonnie and Mij, with our very special cameraman Wolfgang Suschitzky (Su), Director Jack Couffer and of course with Bill, and filming entirely on location (which I always liked best) – the combination of all these created a very special experience. The film was quite loosely based on Gavin Maxwell's book and really focused on the relationship between man and animal (somewhat like *Born Free*), so there was no deep delving into human relationships. But, I believe, the simplicity of the story line was its charm.

Bill's involvement with the film was far more demanding than mine. Quite apart from taking the leading role, he had been asked by Jack Couffer to re-write a lot of the script. It was no mean feat. When filming finished each day he would come back, have supper, and then sit at a desk writing the scene for the next day. It was exhausting and a huge responsibility, and when filming ended he was more than ready for the camping holiday we had planned to take on the Isle of Skye.

Off we all went in our Dormobile (which had served as the wardrobe and changing room for the film and which we had bought) and slowly worked our way north. Our first night was memorable for one reason. Mosquitoes! Mozzie camp we called it. We couldn't wait to leave it! But the next camp, on Skye, was unforgettable for all the right reasons.

Above left: Bill with Mij.

Above right: Louise and Justin with Bambi (No 1).

Right: Bill in Ring of Bright Water.

Below: Sunset over Loch Etive.

Virginia McKenna

We followed the signs to 'The Coral Beach', opened a gate at the end of a grassy track (which we should not have done!), piled some stones across a stream to form a makeshift bridge and, with Bill guiding me, I drove gingerly across to the other side. In a few minutes we were parked on the beach, white sand, shimmering sea, gulls crying and swooping and – silence. Magic. We explored the beach along the coastline, watched curiously by some Highland cattle who were obviously somewhat surprised to see people setting up camp on their territory and, to the children's delight, found a huge log. What fun! It was launched into the water and, with improvised paddles, they manoeuvred it back to our seaside 'home'.

Hours later, eating our supper and looking out to sea, suddenly Bill gasped 'Look, look!', and there right in front of us, splashing in the water, was an otter!

Many years later, in the mid-1990s, the Born Free Foundation participated in an important project on Skye. We'd had a phone call from a lady in Scotland and learned that the tiny island of Eilean Bàn, which nestles beneath the Skye Bridge, was to be sold by auction in Inverness. Will phoned me and we both agreed it would be a tragedy if this was to happen. Who could tell what the island, Gavin Maxwell's last home, would become.

Will contacted the Scottish Office and asked if he could put forward a proposal. Of course we didn't know that the local people were also up in arms about this plan. They had collected some money and were going to go to Inverness to bid at the auction. On arrival, they discovered that the item had been withdrawn by Lord James Douglas-Hamilton, the Scottish Secretary. In due course these local people and ourselves formed the Eilean Bàn Trust, and I took the first of many journeys to Scotland for meetings to determine plans for the island's future.

On Skye itself the Brightwater Centre was also established, housing an information centre, a shop and where wildlife talks and meetings could be held. Here, too, one could buy tickets to go to Eilean Bàn, visit the hide which offered glorious views to other islands, glimpses of seals and birds – and sometimes an otter – and walk up the narrow path through the sensory garden, under the bridge, to the house itself. Formerly lighthouse cottages (one of the treasures of the island is a Stevenson Lighthouse), they had been converted by Maxwell into a lovely home. Dominated by the Long Room, his antique-filled living room where he could, through his telescope, watch the comings and goings on the Skye shore.

Over the years the building had crumbled into disarray and major reconstruction was inevitable. Thanks to the Scottish Office this was done. And thanks to the Harbour Master, the late John MacRae, the restoration of the house and the island environment was set in motion and co-ordinated.

My personal challenge was to try and replicate, as best I could, the extraordinary Long Room. I bought, borrowed and was given various items from generous former colleagues and friends of Maxwell – Raef Payne, Jimmy Watt and John Lister-Kaye in particular. The rest, working from photographs, I tried to find myself. I can't remember how many antique centres I visited. But I do recall how helpful people were when I showed them what I was doing. Perhaps my greatest reward was being able, while I was working, to sometimes stay in the cottage. I never had any evidence of the ghosts they say haunt the place. I only experienced the healing and happiness that nature always brings me.

I love knowing that the Trust is going well, that people still visit the Centre and the Long Room and the hide and, for a short while, can be immersed in the beauty of those skies and changing seas. Even so, I feel the real soul of *Ring of Bright Water* is further south, down the coast, at Sandaig, where Maxwell's first house was built near the shore, the house that burned down and led to him moving to Eilean Bàn. I visited the tiny, one-roomed, whitewashed building still nestling by the wild yellow iris and the beach. I placed my small wildflower tribute on Maxwell's memorial stone, walked across to the other memorial stone where Edal, the otter, is buried under the now-dead rowan tree, and followed the stream to the waterfall, whose sparkling cascades fell with the same energy and brilliance as they did when Maxwell and his human and otter friends bathed in the cold pools beneath. This was Camusfearna. I remembered the Christmas card Bill had received from him after he saw the film. One of Bill's most treasured possessions.

Hands too cold to write at length, but this is just to tell you that Jack Couffer showed me *Ring of Bright Water* last week, and I thought it nothing short of magnificent. What splendid performances you both made, and I think I'm one of the

▶   *Virginia McKenna*

comparatively few people who can appreciate just how difficult it must have been. It is very strange to see on the screen a chunk of one's own life apparently being lived by someone else – but it was so well done that it really seemed like that. In a curious way it's the second time, because Violette Szabo was my pupil and I knew her well.

Do try and visit me here if you ever have time.

Kyle Akin Lighthouse

Isle of Skye

So many times I'd thought,
Imagined, dreamed
Of where the ring
First shimmered in the sun.
And now a greater ring
Encompassed me
As Camusfearna entered in my soul.

A million shells cushioned my eager step
And beckoned me to kneel
And seek the ones
To place upon the graves
With other treasures, gathered from the shore.

It seemed to me
The spirit of those long-gone days
Had touched each fragment
Of that magic place
The dunes, the whispering grass,
The turning tide, the grey-white
Clouds, which architect the sky.

Although I saw no otters swim and play
Their joyous image filled the quiet air
With cries and squeaks which echoed through the hours.
This day, these moments
Are now part of me
Until that time when I will be no more
But spin in space somewhere beyond the stars.

Lark Ascending

OR ME, LOYALTY IS one of the most important human characteristics. It's easy when you are riding high - then people long to join you on the road and smile and wave their mental flags. It is when the going is tough, when there is no 'arm around the shoulder', when your back is against the wall. Such times as these reveal your true friends.

Friendship is a strange thing. What is it that attracts you to another person? Often they have completely different interests, different personalities, different priorities in life. Is it, as Oliver Goldsmith says, 'A disinterested commerce between equals', or, as Byron thought, 'love without wings'? I probably would go for the second, as I don't believe friendship and disinterest make happy companions. I think one does love one's real friends. We are grateful for them, treasure them. They are a gift beyond all else. And the wonderful thing about it, as I have found, is that your husband and your children can also be your friends.

I HEARD a woman's exquisite voice on Radio 4 - *Woman's Hour* - fourteen years ago. I was spellbound. Who is she? She spoke of music and the violin and how she spoke of them affected me in the strangest way. Then, at the end, a fraction of Vaughan Williams' 'Lark Ascending' at once filled the room and my soul. Iona Brown - I knew I admired this person before I ever met her. And I knew that I needed her to do something very special for me: to play 'Lark Ascending' at my funeral. Sounds crazy I suppose, but the soaring birdsong expressed in music by this profound and delightful woman was just what I imagined would be uplifting for my family and friends who will come to wave me goodbye.

I wrote to Iona - and imagine what she did. She phoned our Born Free office - in those days based in a cottage in our garden - and asked if I was seriously ill. She was assured I was absolutely fine and we then spoke on the phone. It was the beginning of a deep and special friendship which ended with Iona's death instead of mine. But she did play at the memorial service for Bill at St James's Piccadilly. The lark's song soared to the roof, as Iona worked her unique magic out of sight up in the organ loft. She didn't want to be seen, she said, the music is what matters. And it did.

> The notes that soared,
> That music on the wing
> Transported all my grief beyond the stars.
>
> And from your magic hands
> A gossamer thread of sound
> Entwined its healing skeins around my heart.
>
> Your spirit too appeared to fly
> Above the heavy walls of church and town
> Into the lark's domain.
>
> How beautiful, how poignant and how rare
> Those fleeting moments when our souls can sing
> And tenderness and love inspire the day.

Iona and her partner, Bjorn Arnils – whom she was later to marry – came with me to Sardinia one summer and shared a peaceful, tranquil week in our house. She floated in the sea – the weightlessness

so soothing for the rheumatoid arthritis which was already invading her body. We laughed and lazed and strolled at evening in the village, enjoying the wine and food and the holiday spirit of timelessness. I see her now – luminous, generous, her smile warming my heart and her passion for music leaving me breathless.

The last time I stayed with her and Bjorn at the house in Bowerchalke she had lost most of her hair as the second tragedy of cancer took hold of her life. But her pain never conquered her. She triumphed over it. Without a sound, in June 2004, she was gone.

It was a strange funeral. I felt she wasn't really there. Somehow, for a person so steeped in music, in all its dimensions, the service seemed to be about someone else. I expected music to fill our hearts as it had hers. But no. Friends and family walked back along the lane to the house, everyone remembering her in their own way. I left the gathering in the garden and went into the sitting room where, a few years before, I had brought my daughter Louise and little grand-daughter Tess to meet her. Tess had played her violin and Iona had listened and talked to her about music and playing. 'Above all', she said, 'you must love it.' Tess was distraught when Iona died.

Sometimes I feel cold and lonely
You've left me alone
All is left of you is
Photographs. Photographs Iona.
When I look outside
Iona all I see is air
When you looked at me Iona
You had droplets in your eyes
Iona we miss you a lot

A lot Iona.
When I was looking forward
To seeing you again
You left me too fast.
Iona, I think of you
All the time. All the time, Iona.

Song written for Iona Brown
Tess, aged nine

Not long ago I heard Alan Titchmarsh on the radio talking about pieces of music that had been very special to him. 'The Lark Ascending' was one. With obvious emotion he described how he had attended a concert given by Iona and how, after playing that heart-stopping music, she had put down her bow for the last time. I, too, have a deeply poignant memory of her, as a conductor. It was a concert in Salisbury Cathedral, and when I went to collect my tickets I was asked if I knew that Iona's mother had died that day. She came on stage unbowed. I ached for her. Later she told me she had done the concert as a tribute to her adored mother. Love triumphs.

Friends and Acquaintances

MAY 3RD. THE MUGUET is late. My hillside lily-of-the-valley holds back its beauty until the sun warms and encourages it to flower. Today it suddenly did seem as if Spring had begun – I walked in the woods with my son Justin and his children and marvelled at the glorious and endless carpet of blue-bells. English, not Spanish! The smell is intoxicating and we poked sticks in leaf-blocked streams and watched excitedly as the trapped water suddenly found its way.

But enjoying, as we always have, our garden and the woods, I remember the marvellous people who have looked after them over the years. Dug out the ditches, chopped logs for the fire, tended the vegetable garden and the flowers, pruned and mowed. Some became friends, and none greater than Dennis Cosham. He worked for the National Trust and came to us in his spare time. From 1964 until his early death in 2002 he was a loyal part of our family, as were his wife Shirley and their children. Somehow, it is always Dennis I see as I wander round: his interest in nature and wild creatures was endearing and the little robin that used to hop trustingly near his spade seemed to know he was safe.

Writing about Iona and Dennis, I began to think of people, outside the family, who have been important, special. In a way, everyone you know is special, so it is hard to choose. George, of course. Kez Wilkins, passionate about animals. Keturah Hain, with whom I enjoy concerts at the Yehudi Menuhin School. Jon and Lou Gardey, two of the most thoughtful people I know. Pamela Hamilton and Toni de Buren, two old comrades from drama school days. My very dear friend, Sally Royds, whom I have known since we were both seven (our mothers were close and played two pianos together). Actress Elizabeth Counsell, whom I met many moons ago when we were in a Sunday charity evening at Drury Lane, and discovered we shared the same birth date – but not the same age! I remember phoning her years ago when we had both been out of work for some while. I had been asked to do a charity evening for the World Wildlife Fund. I suggested to her we did a poetry and music programme together. Libby writes music and

Virginia McKenna

lyrics, plays the guitar and sings like a dream. So, she did the music! *The Lily and the Tiger* had a fairly long life and we took it to little theatres, rooms above pubs and even did a Platform performance at the National Theatre. But more important to me than all that was her generous participation in my mother's funeral service in the little Coldharbour church.

In the latter part of her life my mother's talent as a composer had taken a different direction and she started to compose church music and anthems. They were performed in churches in London, in Antibes and Monte Carlo. Libby played her guitar and sang 'Thank You Lord' – for which my mother had written both words and music. It was so poignant and uplifting, dispelling for a brief moment the sadness of the past days. I was just leaving the house to visit my mother when the phone rang. I was too late. Bill and I went and sat by her – at last her face was free from tension, from all she had inwardly suffered. Her cheek was still warm.

And I have another, much younger friend, Amanda, the daughter of the late Dorothy Tutin and Derek Waring. We'd known the family since the early 1960s when Dottie and I worked in the production of *The Beggar's Opera* with the Royal Shakespeare Company. We kept in touch and in 1969 she and I took our children to Taynuilt near Oban, where we stayed when we filmed *Ring of Bright Water*. Bill and Derek were both working so Dottie and I, together with a lovely young girl who helped us, explored and rowed and swam and had adventures with our little gang, and revelled in the beauty of that glorious coastline. We rented the same house that our family had stayed in before – a large but cosy family house belonging to the charming Nelson family.

So – I have known Amanda and her actor brother Nicky since they were small, but lost touch until about eight years ago. I was in Australia when I got a message asking if I would take Dottie's place in a programme of words and music. Amanda is not only a very talented actress and singer, but has devised most original and entertaining programmes, initially to be performed by her family. Tragically, Dottie's health was deteriorating, and she sometimes was unable to do the show. I started to stand in for her. It was very moving for me: I always felt she was underrated, especially as she got older, and I never really understood why. She had a strong, vibrant personality, wonderful timing and great charisma.

Her family made me very welcome and so much a part of their life. I sat with Derek by her bedside just three days before she died. As beautiful as ever.

Dottie was asked once what she would like to be if she came back in another life. 'A butterfly'. We were at the church in Chichester for her funeral service and those of us who were reading sat on a slightly raised level near the choir stalls. About halfway through the service we saw a beautiful butterfly fluttering above the heads of the assembled gathering, then high up near the ceiling. At the end of the service, the doors at the end were opened, the coffin started its slow journey down the aisle, and the butterfly swiftly flew out into the sunshine. Dottie had her wish. Her spirit was free.

Last year Derek died. It is a strange moment when suddenly you are no-one's daughter or son. He lived very near Amanda and she was a constant presence and support. Nicky, who lived in London, came down whenever he could and, until near the end, Derek used to go and stay with him and his lovely family in London, in the house that had been his and Dottie's. Some dear friends of mine, Rita and Chris, lent me their flat in Minorca and, when all the initial things had been seen to, I took Amanda and her little son Ben there for a week to play and build sandcastles and go on a boat and splash in the pool. She is a big-hearted, warm and spiritual person, continuing to make films about the problems of the elderly in care homes. People without a family, sometimes physically unable to communicate, who have become a shadow of the person they used to be. Isolated, alone, uncherished. It isn't always like that – indeed, the friends who lent me their Minorca flat have a marvellous residential home near Dorking. Proof it can be done.

But the pain of leaving your home, knowing it is 'goodbye to all that', how do you deal with that? I think of GrinGran. I think of my mother. I think of the mother of someone I met who told me how she lived for her garden. Her garden she was leaving forever.

I must remember this
He said
Her hand so pale
Touching the flowers.

Virginia McKenna

Right: Elizabeth Counsell.

Below: As Lucy Lockett, with Derek Godfrey as Macheath and Dorothy Tutin as Polly Peachum in The Beggar's Opera *for the RSC.*

The petals falling
Drifting down
The fingers trembling.
Sweetly. Painfully.

What strength it took
This last farewell
Leaving behind
Treasures so loved.

Engraved forever
Upon his heart
The beauty of flowers
Touched by her love.

A few months ago I was walking in an Autumn garden, still beauti-ful, red apples still clinging to trees, a few faithful flowers bringing a special joy. I was working with Amanda Waring on *Home*, her second film about old people and 'retirement homes'. Like the first (*What Do You See?*) it was based on a poem.

Because this film was being made three years after the first one I felt I related to it more deeply. That could be me. Well, it still could. And if that moment comes I will accept it. I will reach out to that habit I got into when I was in the theatre, making each dressing room into a little 'home'.

I don't think you ever really get away from who you are. 'Oh, go away to get over it,' you hear people say, meaning to offer comfort to someone who has been through a difficult time, or lost someone they loved. You can't just shrug off your sadness or your problem like an old coat. It is with you always, and it is the way you deal with it within your mind and heart that will help you most. And at the end of your life that becomes even more important. Whether you end your life in your own home, someone else's or a 'home'.

Virginia McKenna

Above: Jenny Seagrove with
BFF Rescue Operations Manager
Tony Wiles at Shamwari.

Left: Jill Robinson with the newly
arrived bearcub Ki.

Below: Jill with the bears in their
Sanctuary in Chengdu, China.

The Life in My Years

The moon I love the most
Is not the gleaming ball
Of irridescent light
Sailing the night sky.
The moon I love the most
Rides on the night-dark chests
Of wild black bears,
Sometimes pure white,
Or ivory or cream.
Its crescent marks these beasts
Sublimely. Tragically.

These are the chosen ones
Victims of man's callous need
For cures. Bile in a bottle.
Elixir to end his pain.

But for the trapped moon bears
The pain is endless.
Taps turn. Tubes drip.
The cage an iron glove.
Torment is infinite.

Yet here around me
At the Sanctuary,
There is the sweetest sight.
Bears play and sleep
And shuffle as they will.
They feel the air and smell the rain.
And learn that human-kind
Can be just that.

How humble we should be
To have their trust.
How steadfast we must be
To change men's hearts
So all the crescent moons,
Imprisoned still,
Can shine once more.

Virginia McKenna

The Odd Couple

O F COURSE ANIMALS ARE individuals. I have raised two roe deer, an albino grey squirrel whom we named Sergeant Blanco, and a lion lived in our garden for four months. They each had their own personalities, which we learned to understand and respect, something we had first realised when we made the *Born Free* film. If you are trusted by a wild animal, it is the greatest compliment it can pay you. A relationship not founded on fear.

Bambi No 1 was followed the next year by Bambi No 2. After witnessing the wonderful affinity between Jonnie and the Scottish deer, we shouldn't have been surprised when one afternoon he appeared at the kitchen door holding an infant fawn in his mouth. Holding it so gently. We took it back to the woods, trying to guess where the mother might have left her offspring, hiding among the ferns. But as the evening cooled we brought it back into the house. There are foxes here and the risk of it dying in the night was too great. So another Bambi joined our family. A male, so newly born his hoofs were not quite hard, and he needed feeding every three hours. It was a busy few weeks! He grew. He flourished. He too made friends with Jonnie and together we would walk through the woods and up the field, sometimes accompanied by Macduff, our black cat.

Then Bambi No 2's little horns began to grow and he became quite feisty. We erected a large pen for him in the garden, but I didn't want him to live in a pen on his own indefinitely. So I contacted my forester friend in Staffordshire, who assured me he would be happy to accept another resident in his forest sanctuary. He came down himself, with a friend and a crate, and Bambi No 2 journeyed off to start his new life.

It was this same forester that I phoned after I received a phone call from a neighbour in the village who worked for the fire service in Reigate. A baby albino squirrel had fallen (perhaps been pushed) from a drey high in a tree. Anne Lipscombe had thought of phoning Chessington Zoo but had contacted me instead. I sought advice from the forester about food and all the things I needed to know about squirrels, and I soon realised how little I knew about a squirrel's diet.

I just thought, 'Nuts!' Not at all! Bulbs, roots, winged seeds of maple and sycamore, insect larvae, catkins, orchard fruits, funghi, minerals, the list went on and on. Albino squirrels are rare, and we all waited to see this unusual creature.

The gate opened and Anne appeared carrying a huge laundry basket! She laid it on the path and cautiously opened the lid. Suddenly, there was a flash of white, and I had caught this extraordinarily beautiful and tiny squirrel in my hand, where it snuggled down into my palm. A tail like a translucent egret's feather, eyes of pink alabaster. He - as it turned out to be - was exquisite. We gave him the rather mundane name of Sergeant Blanco but, as it transpired, he was no wilting violet and certainly lived up to his rank! He was accommodated in style. We made his straw bed in a wicker dog basket which had a wire door and left a bowl of food in with him. We watched, fascinated, and then sat quietly as Blanco, having eaten, ventured out to explore his new domain. He climbed all over us and the chairs, finally letting me stroke him and carry him around. That night he went into his straw haven and slept peacefully.

Sergeant Blanco became family without a problem - even sleeping in my son Justin's bed under the bedclothes! Justin, on the other hand, hardly dared move for fear of squashing him! We soon noticed that Sergeant Blanco spent a great deal of time grooming himself. He loved playing with small toys, and his favourite item was a biro pen, which he enjoyed nibbling. Reminding us that metal was on the diet list!

Sadly, indoors was not the right place for Blanco. Fun as it was to see him dash up and down the curtains and leap around the chairs and tables like a fearless acrobat, we knew that he should live outside. Too young yet to release, we bought a large wooden aviary and set it up outside the dining room windows so that we could watch him. We filled it with branches, dishes of food, water, earth and chalky stones, and put straw in the nesting area. He was happy enough in his new quarters.

From dog basket to aviary was a start, but, inevitably, he needed even more space. So we made a taller cage, connected to the aviary by a 'conduit' drainpipe and, again, filled it with big branches. An old wooden letterbox was the 'bedroom'. We weren't sure if he would be too nervous to explore the mysteries of the drain pipe but, never daunted, he disappeared into it, re-emerged inside the cage and

Virginia McKenna

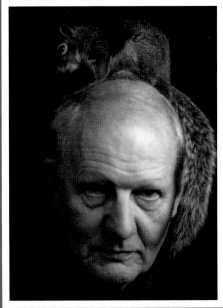

Top left: With Jonnie and Bambi No 2.

Above: Uncle Peter and Diddley, in characteristic pose.

Left: Sergeant Blanco enters the drainpipe.

Below left: Blanco indoors, with Dan and me.

Below right: Blanco the new arrival!

posted himself in the letterbox! Of course, we began to ask ourselves when we could return him to the wild. Would his whiteness make him too vulnerable? But just as we were wondering what to do, another creature came into our lives. A *grey* grey squirrel, Diddley.

I had received a letter from a lady who was caring for a four month old squirrel who lived in her house. His bedroom was a bird cage. Her garden had no trees. She had heard we owned a wood and wondered if she could release Diddley there. 'As soon as you like,' I said.

It was two months after Blanco's arrival. A lovely, warm Sunday. Diddley in his bird cage, his owner, the children and I ventured down the woodland path. It was cool under the dense green canopy as we strolled into the heart of the forest where the ferns were tall and the trees, creepers and shrubs entwined themselves, straining to reach the glimmering light above.

The cage door was opened. For a second the squirrel sat on his owner's shoulder and then he was off, scurrying up the trunk of a tree and disappearing into the topmost branches. We stood quietly, listening to the birdsong, surrounded by the fruits of the forest, and felt it was a good day for him to start his new life. We bid him a hopeful goodbye, but no, it was only *au revoir*.

As it happened, Uncle Peter was staying in the house to look after our dogs and Blanco while I took the children on holiday. Bill was away making a documentary about a lion. One evening Uncle Peter called me. He had been reading peacefully at the dining room table when something jumped on his shoulder. It was Diddley! Poor Uncle Peter nearly died of fright! Simply putting Diddley back in the woods wasn't to be. A temporary solution had to be found until we returned home. So the playroom became Diddley's new territory and he took over Blanco's dog basket. He seemed quite content, hardly ever leaving Uncle Peter's side, particularly when he was playing the piano. He loved to perch on his shoulder or even on his head and listened intently as his new friend played Chopin and Beethoven.

On my return with the children, the playroom got a bit crowded. We decided to give Blanco a companion. For a short time each defended his territory quite aggressively, but in due course they settled down and didn't seem too interested in each other any more.

Mid-September came with its deeper golden sunshine and the promise of autumn rust and yellow. It was a turning point in the seasons and for our squirrels.

Blanco was now strong and agile. We had stopped handling him and we felt the moment had come for the boys to go to their true home, the forest. We called them both into the aviary, blocked up the pipe, moved the cage to the edge of the woodland, cut a hole in its side and inserted a long branch. The other end rested against the trunk of an oak tree. They made their last journey in an old blue canvas bag we had always used for transporting them. Diddley was the first to leave. He found the branch, then the oak tree trunk and, within seconds, he raced upwards. Thirty feet above us he settled down on a branch and promptly fell asleep for about two hours! He was back in his own leafy world.

Blanco was more tentative. He climbed the branch hesitantly and then ran up the oak tree to another branch about 20 feet up. We gazed at him with a mixture of apprehension and encouragement, but suddenly, to our horror, a white spread-eagled shape fell towards us, head, feet and tail extended stiffly in the shape of a six-pointed star. His little body landed with a sickening thud near my feet.

'This is the end,' I thought; 'we should never have let him go.'

Then all at once he got up and ran to a nearby netting fence, climbed halfway up and hung there upside down, breathing very fast. I went and stood by him and a few moments later he climbed onto my shoulder. I stroked him, murmuring reassurances. Then he was off yet again. A little more slowly he climbed up into the sun-dappled shadows. I watched him weaving his way up and down, as he forged his way deeper and deeper into the forest until he disappeared. At half-past five Diddley awoke and followed Blanco's aerial pathway to freedom. They were both gone.

Autumn came, leaves were gathered for compost; the trees, bare once more, formed crazy tangled shapes and the sky was visible again, even from the densest part of the woods.

Now and again a very friendly squirrel approached quite close when we were gardening. It could have been Diddley! And then, just before Christmas, two different people phoned and told us they had seen a white squirrel in the woods which border the road leading into Dorking.

It was snowing. Trying not to remember my reputation as the world's worst photographer, I grabbed my camera ('sunny bright', 'dull shadowy', 'dark gloomy'), piled on layers of clothes and set off for the top woods. I settled myself near a forestry gate. Three hours passed. Suddenly, only five or six feet away, that flash of white! Blanco ran up the nearest tree. I had found him, or had he found me? I took about six pictures and then we travelled along together, he in his tree world and I along the silent road of snow. Calling his name and calling goodbye. That was the first of several meetings over almost four years.

Bill, an excellent photographer, went into the woods one day with our son Daniel. They strolled along, singing, whistling and calling. Blanco suddenly appeared again, strong and agile and beautiful. I now knew, without question, that it had in fact been right to let him return to his own environment, instead of being a loved but inappropriate visitor in ours.

Shocked into the Present

I WANT TO TELL YOU about the lion who lived in our garden, but I can't. Not yet. It's May 2008, and my mind and my heart are completely overwhelmed by the tragedies in Burma and China. The cyclone, the earthquake, natural disasters on such a scale difficult for us to believe possible, had we not seen it on the television news.

Burma, or I should say Myanmar, the land of beautiful, gentle people, torn apart; families, animals, fields all drowned, homes ripped open, buildings crumbled. Loss of life estimated, as I write, reaching almost 50,000. Hundreds of thousands of other people displaced, starving, wounded. No food, fresh water, or medical aid. It would have torn Bill in two. At last, today, some outside help is being allowed in. But too little and, for so many people, too late.

Are there no moments, events, in our world where politics, suspicion and hostility are forgotten? In the face of such tragedies as these, can't the leaders put aside politics and simply be human beings? 'Do as you would be done by' seems a reasonable start.

China is no less a victim. It is expected that over 60,000 people will have died in the earthquake and more than four million homes are in ruins. With so many schools destroyed it is feared that thousands of China's children were killed. Families with only one child suddenly have none. The thought is unbearable. How do you rebuild your life? Can you?

If I were a few years younger I would have volunteered to go out and help in some way, joining my friend Jill, and the Animals Asia team. But at least one can respond to the pleas for financial support and give what one can.

One poignant report was of a school, cut in half. The body of a small girl lay on the top floor, her little pink trousered legs dangling over the edge. She was crying, alive for four days, helplessly watched by her parents who were pleading and shouting for help. None came. The little legs that had been moving, moved no more. Just how can one deal with that?

Hundreds of thousands of deaths. And now the single death of a friend, who wasted away from asbestosis. Jim was the much-loved partner of one of my closest friends, Penny Grosjean, whose mother Therese had looked after our family when we first arrived in Kenya in 1964. Already, in February, when I saw them in Perth on my visit to Australia, he was ill, losing weight and energy. But the disease hurtled through his body in the following three months and last week one of the kindest, most thoughtful, unassuming people you could meet was gone.

My heart went out to Penny, who had looked after her second husband until his death. Although she appears strong and resilient, I have always sensed a deep vulnerability. She pays me the greatest compliment by allowing this side of her to show when we are together. And she knows there is always a room in my home for her.

One thing we know
One thing is sure
That we must die
And be no more.

Into the dark
Of grave and ground
Where there's no light
Where there's no sound.

What will you say
When I am gone
What will you tell
Our little son?

Speak not of worms
Of cold and clay
Of sightless eyes
And heart's decay.

Let him remember
Warmth and joy
While he is still
A little boy.

It was our mutual love of Africa that brought Penny and me together. How she would have adored to meet the lion in our garden!

Virginia McKenna

Christian the Lion

I T WAS 1969. TWO young Australians, Anthony (Ace) Bourke and John Rendall, visited the pet department at Harrods just before Christmas. There, in a small cage, were two lion cubs. The boys were transfixed. Somehow they raised the money, found an understanding landlord, and took the male cub home. Christian came to Chelsea.

A few months later Bill and I drove up to London. He needed a pine desk for an old gypsy caravan we had in the garden, and I was going to my dressmaker, Anthony. We parked near The Church of St John in the Parish of the World's End, Chelsea, and agreed where to meet later. In bygone times it was, indeed, the end of the world. Beyond lay 'the wilds', inhabited by highwaymen, but in 1970 it was abuzz with shops and cafés. I emerged from my fitting, but there was no sign of Bill, neither in 'Granny Takes a Trip' - fondly reassuring us that it's not only youth that counts, nor in 'Gandalf's Garden', decorated with Maharishi-type faces and sitar music drifting out of the open door. Anthony proffered the information that he might be in 'Sophistocat', the furniture shop.

'Why?' I asked.

'Oh, don't you know, they've got that animal in there. With spots and stripes or something.'

'Difficult to have both,' I puzzled.

'Oh well, it's got teddy bear ears,' he laughed.

Suddenly all was clear!

I rushed to Sophistocat. Through the door I watched Bill and two young men moving things off a table, on which a young lion was padding about before finally flopping down. I went in. His amber-coloured eyes watched me as I stroked his head. I was in heaven.

It seemed we had arrived on the scene at a very opportune moment. Christian was growing fast. Exercising him in the nearby Moravian Close, by kind permission of the vicar, was becoming a problem, as the games of football enjoyed by the boys and Christian were becoming more boisterous. In the shop too, Christian was obliged to spend more time in the basement, away from customers.

John and Ace didn't want him to go to a zoo or safari park, but knew something had to be done, fast.

I knew, without a shadow of doubt, as we drove home, that Bill was already hatching a plan. Christian, before long, would be part of our lives. He asked the boys if they would agree to allow Christian to be rehabilitated in the wild, in Kenya. If permission from the government could be obtained and if George Adamson would be willing to do it. (I think we already knew the answer to that!)

It was an irresistible idea, and before we knew it, James Hill (director of *Born Free* who still worked with Bill) and ourselves were filming a re-enactment of that first encounter at Sophistocat. It was the only scene that had to be reconstructed. By the time the hoped-for permission had come through, Christian would probably have grown bigger.

To our delight the Kenyan government agreed to the scheme – though I imagine a few heads shook in disbelief at the thought of a 'British' lion coming to Kenya. Locating a suitable area was more of a problem. Weeks passed. A worried phone call to Bill from John alerted us to the fact that Christian could no longer be kept in London. Could we help?

It took four days to erect a lion compound in our garden, enclosing an area of 400 square yards, with an overhang atop the eighteen-foot high fence and a double gate. The gypsy caravan, minus a desk, was placed inside to serve as Christian's night quarters. The former home of a King of the Road would now shelter the King of Beasts.

We drove the Dormobile to World's End and, together with the boys, the young lion took the first steps on the safari that we hoped would end in Africa. We made sure that the children and the dogs were in the house, and walked Christian through the garden to his new home. He padded round examining the shrubs, the trees and the caravan and we stood around for some while, to establish that the territory belonged to us all.

The children loved watching him, running back and forth to report on everything he did. The dogs' reactions were fascinating, all different. Jonnie longed to have a game! Our old poodle, Boy, defended what he thought was his territory (outside the wire!) and kept up his barking for quite some time. Nell, our collie, whom we had brought back with us from Kenya, maintained a respectful distance under a May tree – occasionally coming up to nudge me if I sat by the wire talking to Christian for too long. Macduff, the cat, took no notice at all, much more interested in the mice in the meadow than another cat!

It was a magical Spring and Summer. Blossoms, bluebells, yellow azaleas, the scent of flowers was heady. Christian's owners John and Ace lived in a small caravan near the enclosure. Fine for a couple of weeks, but as the weeks turned into months it became very difficult.

Bill carried on filming as we all waited for more news, returning to Kenya to help George, who was still trying to find an area for the new camp. Back home, the boys continued to play with Christian, always thinking of new ways to keep him interested and active.

One very special day we arose at 3.30 am. By 5 am we stood on the beach at West Wittering in the pale dawn light. Christian was let off his leash and we raced over the brightening sand to the water's edge. A quick paw-dip in the sea was enough for him and he sped off with us in hot pursuit, all of us finally flopping down to rest and regain our breath. It was a moment to remember, the old, weathered brown and seaweed-green breakwaters, the sea-smoothed sand, the sensations of childhood, half-forgotten but still tangible, sharing those few moments of freedom with a lion on an English beach. Far away we saw a lady walking her dog. Christian's leash was back on promptly and we quietly went back to the vehicle and drove home.

It was another three and a half months before we finally got the longed-for news. I felt a strange mixture of sadness and joy, but there was little time to think about anything except preparations for the journey. The travelling crate had already been in the enclosure for several weeks so Christian could get used to it, but scales had to be borrowed so he could be weighed, advice sought from expert, Oliver Graham-Jones, on tranquilisation, insurance arrangements made. (We were to film on the tarmac at Heathrow, and we had to insure the airport for one million pounds!)

It was raining the day Christian finally left our home. He went into his crate happily and ate the pieces of meat into which the sedative had been inserted, a mild tranquiliser just to keep him calm, not to make him sleep. We set off for the airport in convoy, the children following with some of our friends.

On the tarmac, the crate was raised on a fork-lift truck and gradually disappeared into the shadows of the hold. None of us spoke, but I know we were thinking of Christian in the darkness without his 'family'.

Above: Christian the lion outside the gypsy caravan in our garden where he slept.

Right: Both of us with Christian, John (left) and Ace (right).

Below: All of us on the beach at West Wittering, Sussex.

Virginia McKenna

Above: Christian in the crate at Heathrow, ready to fly to Nairobi.

Below: Tension as Christian (left, behind George's legs) meets Boy (right) for the first time.

I said goodbye to Bill, John and Ace, and joined the children. We watched the plane, a silver-gold streak in the evening sun, soar up and out of sight.

Later, all was quiet at home. The deserted enclosure was as desolate as an empty fairground when the roundabouts are still and the music no longer plays. Christian's old play sack looked, for a moment, like some child's abandoned rag doll. The gypsy caravan was no longer a sleeping room. 'I must try and find a writing desk,' I thought, 'before Bill gets home.' I went back to the house to seek the comfort of being with my own little 'pride'.

No-one knew better than George Adamson how long it takes to return a lion to a wild life: between eighteen months and two years. It was the start of a new life not only for Christian but also for George and Boy (one of the lions in *Born Free* whose rehabilitation in Meru Game Reserve had its problems). Introducing Christian to Boy was one of the main challenges George, Bill and the boys had to face. Bill knew how I would be anxiously awaiting news and kept me regularly informed.

The heat during the journey was intense. Relentless. Dry, arid thornbush country, stony tracks, seams of lava dust. Christian's thick coat became a mantle of misery.

As the 280 mile journey came to an end, the hostile terrain began to change as the life-giving Tana river allowed palm trees and bushes and lush undergrowth to flourish. Cooling. Soothing. I wondered so much how Christian was coping. Bewildered at first, I was told, but overjoyed by the freedom, and instinctively aware of all the new sights and sounds and smells. His wild instincts may have been dulled but they were certainly still at work. And there was much to learn. He must establish his territory and defend it, to hunt, to live in a pride. But, first, he had to meet Boy.

On this issue no progress had been made, but George finally decided that the moment could be delayed no longer. Boy lay, magnificent, on the top of a rocky outcrop. Christian and his human friends slowly made their way towards him. As they approached Boy rose, enormous and threatening. Only about five yards separated them when Boy charged. Paws flew through the air, dust swirled, roars resounded, Christian flung himself on his back in submission. Suddenly it was quiet. Boy moved away. Christian remained crouching, making a strange snarling sound. The confrontation had lasted only a few minutes but to George, Bill, Ace and John it seemed forever.

Mercifully, Christian was unhurt. The pecking order had been established and it was the start of an amazing, close and wonderful friendship between Boy and Christian, so brilliantly captured in artist Gary Hodges' drawing below.

I can imagine the agony John and Ace felt at parting from Christian. I can feel it. It never leaves you, but entwined with the sadness are the riches of the experience of being close to a wild animal. The privilege of that and the realisation that, if you really love and understand, you let go. They returned nine months later and the emotional reunion with Christian was, miraculously, caught on film. Heartstopping. Bill's documentary *Christian: The Lion at World's End* is one of his most unusual and finest.

Christian was now, finally, a true wild lion, occasionally returning to visit George. But in 1973 he disappeared for the last time. George felt a great sadness but also that perhaps the moment had come for his friend to go off and establish his own life, his own pride. He had certainly learned the skills to do that.

As for the rest of us at home, the part of my garden where Christian lived will always be a special place. The trees and shrubs are taller, the grass longer, the wild flowers more profuse, but the memory of Christian is as strong as ever.

Dark Times

EVERYONE MARKS THEIR BIRTHDAY in a different way. Christian's first birthday present was a large 'cake' made of minced meat. How he enjoyed it! Some people just *have* to have a party - friends, food, music, dressing up. A real festive occasion. I always loved to do parties or treats for the children when they were young and, usually, a small dinner party for Bill, and he took me out for a meal and to the theatre. But neither of us really went in for making birthdays big events, except for cards and a gift. Just to remember the moment.

When Bill died, my eldest son Will gave me a very special birthday. He knew how the first of all the 'anniversaries' are hard to get through. He took me to a tapas restaurant in Hammersmith in London and then we went to Cirque du Soleil. The most wonderful circus in the world, with not an animal in sight. I was entranced.

My 77th birthday, almost two weeks ago, was very different. My aunt Colette (my uncle John's widow), in Nîmes, was to be 90 years old the day before and my cousin, Johnny, who lives in France and his eldest daughter, Ann, my god-daughter, and I had arranged to go to Nîmes and take her out to lunch. We all arrived on the Friday, Ann from Zürich, and on the Saturday we took her to lunch in a delightful family restaurant, recommended by the florist from whom I'd bought Colette some gorgeous peonies. It was perfect. The young waiter advising us and guiding us through the menu with colourful and engaging descriptions of the ingredients. Even the vegetarian food was brilliant - not so common in France! We lingered over our meal and finally left at about 3.30 pm, Johnny preferring to sit in the square with his coffee whilst we shop-gazed for a while.

The narrow lanes of Nîmes are intriguing, lined with colourful shops of all kinds and dotted by squares where cafés and enticing patisseries tempt you with delicious cakes. Irresistible! Now and then a beautiful cool-walled church confronts you as you turn a corner and a clock chimes the hour. At the north end of the lanes there is an indoor food market where I had often been with Colette. Nowhere in England can shops match the way the French display their produce -

Colette at home.

cheeses, fruits and vegetables, breads and flowers to feast your eyes. This time we didn't venture into that aromatic world. At 4 o'clock we went our different ways until early evening, Colette to go home, I to my hotel and Johnny and Ann to stay at the café watching the world go by.

As I opened my hotel room door the phone was ringing. Colette. She'd had a bad fall in the street near her flat. I raced round. Never have I seen so much blood, nor such bruising. Her whole face and neck were deep crimson, her lip swollen and cut, her fingers and one knee were bleeding profusely. Not to mention the shock of it all. A kind passer-by walking her dog had brought her upstairs and had called a friend, whose son was a surgeon, and who quickly arrived to take us to the clinic. Within half an hour Colette was in a room on the bed. I telephoned my cousin and Ann. It was horrendous.

But my aunt really showed her true colours. She hardly complained, made no big deal about her wounds or the stitches but apologised to us for having 'spoiled' the visit. It was very touching. I'm sure her strength of character helped her through the pain and chaos of the accident, but strong people find it difficult not to be in total control, and she was reluctant to let Ann and me out of sight in the kitchen as we prepared supper! I moved in from the hotel and stayed with her for the next two nights. By the time Monday came a little rota of helpers was at work.

Yet the dark clouds over this birthday had not yet passed. They darkened.

I arrived home late in the afternoon and went down to my office. Suddenly Will appeared at the door. 'You're back early,' I said. I knew something had happened. 'I have to tell you that Rita died on Saturday,' he said. I couldn't take it in. Wonderful Rita and Chris (who had lent me the flat in Minorca) had come over for a drink on Thursday evening to bring me birthday presents. We had looked at the ponies in the field, we'd talked and laughed and chatted about an event, a Ball in Derby, we were all going to later in the month.

Rita and Chris were regular members of the little group I had been taking to East Africa on safari for the past few years. They had fallen in love with the wildlife, the people and were the first to be thinking about the next trip before the last one was over! When I gave up the safaris they organised the 2007 one on their own. And this was to continue. I'm not sure about this year.

Rita lit up whatever world she walked into. Always giving out, caring, with an unquenchable passion for animals. She lived life to the full, to the end. And the end was on my birthday. One day comes when you breathe out and then – you don't breathe in.

'Why fear death? It is the most beautiful adventure in life.' Charles Frohman, 1860–1915 (last words before going down in *The Lusitania*).

My friends on safari in Amboseli: Chris and Rita are fifth and sixth from left.

BACK TO the earth. Back to nature. At the end of my garden, towards the woods, are the little graves of some of our beloved dogs, our cat, my son Dan's two cats and a goose. Part of my life still.

I was attending an event at the Royal Geographical Society in London, when someone asked me which book had been a major influence on me. My answer was unequivocal: *Wild Animals I Have Known*, by Ernest Thompson Seton. My father gave it to me when I was a child, together with *Black Beauty* and *Jock of the Bushveldt*. Only now, writing this, am I suddenly conscious that my father might have sensed an as-yet unarticulated side of my nature. My feelings for animals.

Seton wrote:

We and the beasts are kin. Man has nothing that the animals have not at least a vestige of; the animals have nothing that man does not in some degree share. Since, then, the animals are creatures with wants and feelings differing in degree only from our own, they surely have their rights.

For Seton the individuality of the animal was paramount. I'm sure this is why I was instinctively drawn to him. 'Those who do not know the animals well,' he writes, 'well may think I have humanised them, but those who have lived so near them as to know somewhat of their ways and their minds will not think so.'

What a magical evening it would have been to sit with Seton, Bill and George around a camp fire. In the warm, still night of Africa or in the rolling hills of England, or on a wild deserted beach on the west coast of Scotland – no matter where. To sit with people who really understand the ways of animals, through watching, waiting, listening, and do all these with a deep humility.

From an early age, I immersed myself in Seton's tales of Raggylug the cottontail rabbit, Lobo the grey wolf, Silverspot the crow, Wully the sheepdog and all the rest, and each evening I dissolved in tears. As Seton says, 'The life of a wild animal always has a tragic end'. Yes, that is true. A 'ripe old age' is rarely the lot of an animal in the wild. And it is true too for captive wild creatures as well – though in a different way. They may have a long life but it is a wasted life. And that too is a tragedy.

One Lucky Break after Another!

THEY SAY THAT IF you are a Gemini you have a split personality. I'm not much into self-analysis, but I am at ease in different worlds. Perhaps the link is an urge to understand living beings - whether people or animals. It is essential to connect with others as an actress and, of course, vital in the second world I have dipped into, the world of animals.

Both worlds are fascinating, demanding, enriching. Both require you to give of yourself. As an actor you are the only tool you have and this requires you to overcome reserve and, sometimes, allow emotions to show through the character you are playing that you would hesitate to show in 'real' life.

I have often been asked if I prefer acting on stage or in films. An almost impossible question to answer! Instinctively I would say the theatre is my greatest love. The immediacy, the danger, the subtle changes you are able, over time, to introduce into your performance, the relationships with your fellow actors and with the audience. The 'Beginners on stage' call always produced an extra heartbeat. For what might lie ahead in the next few hours?

For me, whichever medium I have worked in, the foundation and creation of the character lies within myself. The feelings, the thoughts, the emotions have to be true. On film, the camera can find your soul; on stage you have to project it. For me, that is the main difference. I do find filming rewarding: the subtlety, the 'less is more', I love that. Obviously, there is less freedom in a studio. You are dependent on so many other people and the value of a good director can't be exaggerated. The discipline is huge, the concentration, the deep understanding of your character is essential, so that whether you are doing a scene at the end or the middle, before you have done the beginning, it doesn't matter. You know who you are. Where you are.

IN BOTH theatre and films I have had the good fortune to work with some of the most talented and inspirational actors. In my entire

Virginia McKenna

career I met only two who were less than generous in their attitude. This is so rare. All actors know how difficult it is, and so normally there is a wonderful team spirit and camaraderie.

I was also lucky to train at the Central School of Speech and Drama, now at Swiss Cottage. But in the 1940s, when I was there, its home was the Royal Albert Hall. When we didn't have a class we were allowed to creep into the vast auditorium and listen to rehearsals. It was magic. As you can imagine, our school theatre was an unusual shape, following the curve of the building, very wide and very shallow. Quite an acting challenge, but I was happy there. Our distinguished teachers included Cicely Berry, now of Royal Shakespeare Company fame, and our understanding and clever Principal, Gwynneth Thurburn.

At the end of my second year an agent, Kenneth Carten, who had seen me in a School production, got me two plays at Dundee Rep, *Black Chiffon* and *Northanger Abbey*, during the summer break. I never returned to School for the third year, instead joining the company for the next ten plays and enjoying the challenge and fun of working in a company and getting my first pay packets. Dundee was fortnightly rep, and I earned £6.50 a week, of which £4 went on my digs' rent. Although I was only there for six months, it was one of the most valuable training grounds I could have hoped for.

It was while I was playing Estella in a production of *Great Expectations* that Daphne Rye, the talent scout for H M Tennent, came to Dundee. She was on a tour of the reps. Unfortunately I had developed the most awful boil on my face, so I must have presented a less than appealing Estella! I couldn't believe it when I heard that she had gone back to London and suggested me for the part of Dorcas in a new play by John Whiting, *A Penny for a Song*. The boil hadn't mattered!

Goodbye to my Dundee friends and Arthur Whatmore who ran the theatre, and the first steps on a career which would continue for the next fifty or so years, slowly diminishing, however, as I delved deeper into the animal world.

A Penny for a Song, directed by Peter Brook, was at the Haymarket in London and the cast was awesome: Ronald Squire, Basil Radford, George Rose, Denis Cannan and gracious Marie Lohr. To my amazement I discovered she had known my father and, on the first night, she gave me a beautiful pendant of enamel and gold that my father had given to her.

Top left: As Perdita in A Winter's Tale, *with Richard Gale as Florizel.*

Above: With Donald Sinden in The Cruel Sea.

Below: In The Barretts of Wimpole Street, *with Bill, Jennifer Jones and John Gielgud.*

The Smallest Show on Earth

Above: With the main cast – Margaret Rutherford, Bill, director Basil Dearden, Peter Sellers, Bernard Miles and Leslie Phillips.

Below and right: Leslie, Bill and I see the cinema for the first time...

In those days one would never address the senior members of the cast by their first names. There was a deep sense of respect and courtesy. I was in awe of these actors, and of 'treading the boards' in such a famous theatre.

The set was designed by Emett and, naturally, was exquisitely eccentric. As were the characters in the story. I shall never forget Marie Lohr's delivery of the line 'Shut the gate!', as a large cannonball rolled through it onto the stage where everyone was sitting around having a picnic, while George Rose scanned the horizon for invaders through his telescope from a treetop perch. Her stentorian tone resonated with Edith Evans' Lady Bracknell's 'A handbag?!' in *The Importance of Being Ernest*. Theatrical and unmatchable treasures.

My friends in the cast were Ronald Howard (Leslie Howard's son), who played the blind soldier with whom Dorcas fell in love, and Peter Martin. Sometimes we went to the famous Buckstone Club opposite the stage door of the theatre for a meal and a drink. It was here that I was introduced to Merrydown cider. I had no idea of its potency and one evening I foolishly drank two glasses! My head spinning, I felt completely 'out of it' and on the next day had the headache of a lifetime. No more head-down Merrydown for me!

Life was good to me. It was a heady time in other ways. I was going from theatre to film to television with little or no break in between, sometimes filming in the day and playing in the theatre in the evening. Tiring but exhilarating.

In 1951 I did a film at Elstree called *Father's Doing Fine*. I played, rather inappropriately, a young woman, Catherine, who resorted to the gin bottle to ease her woes (although I suppose the Merrydown experience came in useful!). How I longed to play the tomboy part that Susan Stephen had been given, and to wear jeans and shirt instead of the figure-hugging pink velvet evening dress I was 'poured' into. The film also featured Jack Watling, Richard Attenborough, Brian Worth and Heather Thatcher. Perhaps one we are all happy to bury in the mists of time.

But in that same year I played Perdita in Shakespeare's *A Winter's Tale* – again directed by Peter Brook – with John Gielgud, Diana Wynyard and Flora Robson. There was one performance when I had the privilege of seeing, close up, the willpower of an actor in action. In the play the Queen, Hermione, played by Diana Wynyard, has withdrawn from the world for sixteen years, following the cruel and unsubstantiated jealous accusations made by her husband, Leontes. At the end of the play Hermione is revealed as a statue (living of course) before the final reconciliation with Leontes, and her meeting with her daughter, Perdita.

I never tired of watching Diana Wynyard, truly statue-like, seeming not to breathe. Such incredible control. Then, one night, I saw her eyes fill with tears and her throat contract as she desperately tried not to cough. The eyes of the audience and the actors were fixed on this beautiful motionless woman who dared not tremble or swallow or show, in any way, that she was a living being. How she will have longed for Paulina to say the line 'You perceive she stirs!' Then, at last, she could live again and never has a greeting between husband and wife and mother and daughter been more warmly felt!

Richard Gale was Florizel, and he and I spent many anxious moments at the side of the stage, having been made acutely aware of the inadequacies of our Shakespearean 'delivery'. It was John Gielgud who restored our confidence, just by talking to us and encouraging us. A man of such generosity and kindness. I had the great good fortune to work with him again in the film of *The Barretts of Wimpole Street*. He was Mr Barrett, Jennifer Jones played Elizabeth and Bill was Robert Browning. I was the naughty Henrietta who was always in trouble with Papa. In one scene he had to take my wrists and force me to my knees. After we had finished he apologised so sweetly in case he had hurt me, which, of course, he hadn't. In any case, I was all for a bit of realism!

There is a very particular delight in working with people more than once. It happened many times with Bill, and three times with Gielgud, but also with Pamela Brown and Paul Scofield. She and I had been in an experimental film at the Riverside Studios in 1951, *The Second Mrs Tanqueray* by Pinero with Hugh Sinclair. I'm not sure if the experiment was successful or if many people ever saw it. The 'takes' were endlessly long, twelve to fifteen minutes. Four cameras worked in a rota, each taking over from the other as we walked about on the one large set. So my introduction to film-making was completely different from the experiences I was to have later.

Not so much later as it turned out. *The Cruel Sea*, with Jack Hawkins, Donald Sinden (whose girlfriend I played), Denholm Elliott, Stanley Baker and a host of other top actors, was the real beginning of my film career. My part as Julie Hallam was small, but the Wren's hat was unforgettable it seems, as so many people have remarked on it over the years! It wasn't until I saw the completed film that I really understood the power of the story and the brilliance of some of the performances, especially that of Jack Hawkins; the subtle way in which emotions were expressed, the understatement. But even in the less dramatic and emotional moments I was acutely aware of how much a good director can bring to a scene. Charles Frend gave you confidence, the most needed ingredient of all when you are starting out and was unfailingly courteous. It was the first time I had to kiss someone in a film and I was extremely nervous. Donald was sweet and considerate, but I suppose I felt gauche and insecure. A year later in *The Ship that Died of Shame*, playing George Baker's wife, I had gained confidence and felt much more relaxed. For some reason I was asked to watch that film a couple of years ago and I found myself comparing the scene George and I did together to the love scenes we see today. Whether the scene is in a crowded room, on a road, in bed, or a railway station, the essence has to be in the feeling, the chemistry between the actors, the things that are not said. Of course, our scene was of its time. Understated, sweet, poignant and, I hope, touched hearts. I worked with George again, many years later, in one of his Ruth Rendell mystery series. The same kind, generous actor.

The Passionate Summer

The film Bill and I made for Rank in Jamaica in 1958, when I was expecting our first child – struggling with the heat and morning sickness!

Virginia McKenna

Carve Her Name with Pride

I N 1965 WARIS HUSSEIN directed a TV production of *A Passage to India* for the BBC, with the inimitable Sybil Thorndike playing Mrs Moore. We were all in awe in the early days of rehearsal and one morning Waris asked her, very tentatively, if she could do a particular move.

'Of course,' she replied; 'Just tell me what you would like me to do.'

A director's dream and, of course, Waris knew that whatever he asked her to do she would illuminate with her own inner light. Something that can't be taught. You either have it or you don't.

Paul Scofield definitely had it. I first became aware of this gift in actors while playing in *The River Line* by Charles Morgan. Again an outstanding cast with Pamela Brown, Robert Hardy, Marjorie Fielding, Michael Goodliffe, John Westbrook and Paul. We played at the Edinburgh Festival in the early 1950s and then came to London. There is a key characteristic that really great actors seem to share, and that is modesty. Bill recognised this characteristic in Paul when they worked at Stratford in 1962. Sometimes he and Paul would have a meal together and talk. I know Bill admired him enormously – as a person, not only as an actor. He felt that Paul was inspirational on many levels, and asked him one day if he had ever thought of becoming a director. (How exciting it would be to be directed by someone of such intelligence, awareness and sensitivity). Paul didn't think he wanted to take that road, Bill said. He just wanted to act.

Paul was an actor you couldn't take your eyes off. I worked with him again in 1957 in the film *Carve Her Name with Pride*, which tells the story of Violette Szabo who was executed for spying for the Allied forces during World War II. A film of huge emotions, demanding total commitment to the real people we were interpreting. Often I couldn't 'cut off' at the end of the day's filming. But, thank heaven, we had the most sensitive, honest and discriminating of directors, Lewis Gilbert.

I think all of us involved in the Violette Szabo story were affected by it in a lasting way. The sacrifices made by such courageous people working in Europe behind enemy lines are almost incomprehensible to us. Could we, would we have done the same? In Violette's case leaving her little daughter, Tania, with her mother and father to face the dangers and uncertainties of living under a false identity, knowing what would happen if you were caught.

Violette's marriage to Etienne, who was in the French Foreign Legion, was ecstatically happy but cruelly brief. He was killed in North Africa. El Alamein, a name synonymous to us with that of General Montgomery. The story of what happened to Violette was first told by R J Minney in his book from which the film took its title. That book was an invaluable reference, filling out events, descriptions, relationships that, inevitably, were touched on more briefly within the confines of the script.

My most treasured source of information and understanding, however, was Odette Hallowes. The first woman to be awarded the George Cross (which Violette received posthumously). She too had been in Special Operations Executive (SOE) and had been captured by the Germans in 1943. She was first sent to the infamous Fresnes prison in Paris, from there to the Avenue Foch, where she was brutally tortured, and then moved to Ravensbrück and condemned to death. She was at Ravensbrück at the same time as Violette, but she survived and was able, after the war, to give some information about what had happened to Violette.

Few could imagine what it is like to listen to the personal stories of someone who had lived through such terrifying times. I was only an actress playing a part, the part of a young woman who had endured similar horrors but had not survived. Little wonder that the story of making the film made a deep impression on me. One I keep to this day.

Odette was a quiet, modest person, profound and fun as well. And a realist. She told me that when she was in prison she realised how little one really needs in life. Staying alive was the most important thing. So, she decided that if she got out she would have just one dress, copied in different fabrics and colours. Life would be simple. When she did become free and returned to England it didn't take long for her to admit that such a simple philosophy wasn't really practical!

Thinking of dresses, a flashback to 1944. Just before returning to England after her first mission, Violette went shopping in Paris. She visited Molyneux in the Rue Royale. Molyneux, the couturier, where

Virginia McKenna

Above: With Paul Scofield on the set of Carve Her Name with Pride.

Right: With director Lewis Gilbert, Odette Hallowes and Paul on set.

Bottom left: With Maurice Ronet.

Bottom right: With Nicole Stéphane as Denise Bloch and Anne Leon as Lilian Rolfe.

my aunt Marguerite was the Directrice before, during and after the war. She could have met Violette! She could well have!

The muddy banks and ditches on the lot at Pinewood Studios were crowded but silent. Figures in striped prison clothes dug and hacked at the ground without speaking. Saving their energy for the task they were forced to do if they wanted to avoid punishment. It no longer felt like a film. We had been working for three and a half months and illusion had almost become reality. Only a few more days and we would be filming the execution by firing squad of Violette and her colleagues and friends Denise Bloch and Lilian Rolfe. We were filthy, exhausted but always alert to the intimidating presence of the guards. Lewis had, with the greatest understanding and sensitivity, scheduled these scenes for the end. We had come a long way from Violette's happy early days in Brixton to her tragic death at Ravensbrück. It was Lewis who supported me when I said I felt totally unable to face the executioners with a smile on my face. The powers-that-be had requested this and I found it completely out of character and unacceptable. So, there was no smile.

As actors in the story I believe we had travelled too. Although I had no children of my own then, I deeply felt the grief of saying goodbye to little Tania and 'my' parents for what might be, and indeed was, the last time. Acting is almost undefinable. As an artist you have a palette and a paintbrush; as a musician you have an instrument; as a dancer you have gruelling training and dancing shoes. As an actor you have yourself. You are the instrument, the paintbrush, the dancing shoes. Yes, you can learn to move well, project your voice, study technique and timing, but in the end it is your accumulated understanding of life and emotions that helps you in the parts you play. In *Carve Her Name with Pride* the experience was huge and varied and sometimes overwhelming. It was about someone who had really lived and really died, and because of that it is one of the two films that are still a part of me.

There is a little jewel at the heart of this story. A poem. Written by Codemaster Leo Marks and given by him to Violette to use as her code poem. From 1958 until the present day this poem has been read, spoken and remembered by thousands of people. Over the years I have been asked to say it at funerals, memorial services and, most important to me, at the annual gathering in Wormelow, Herefordshire, where a museum was established in June 2000 in Violette's memory.

The house in the grounds used to be owned by Violette's aunt and uncle and she would go there for holidays. Now lived in for the past 45 years by Rosemary Rigby MBE. She became intensely aware of the spirit of Violette which appeared to lighten every corner of this country garden and determined to create a lasting memorial to this awe-inspiring young woman. At the opening of the museum it was filled with what I call the 'real' people. Tania Szabo, her daughter, Leo Marks, the Codemaster, a contingent of war veterans humbly wearing their medals and some SOE survivors paying their personal tribute to a remarkable and brave young woman. Some of them had known and worked with her.

At this gathering the poem, for me, is always the centre – carrying, as it does, the history between its birth over 65 years ago and the present day. It is a love poem in its profoundest sense. That is why I always carry this little 'jewel' in my heart.

The life that I have
Is all that I have
And the life that I have
Is yours

The love that I have
Of the life that I have
Is yours and yours and yours

A sleep I shall have
A rest I shall have
Yet death will be but a pause

For the peace of my years
In the long green grass
Will be yours and yours and yours.

Leo Marks (1943)

Sea Change

IT IS A STRANGE feeling writing about my days as an actress. It is, if I'm honest, like another life. The last time I worked in the theatre - in the musical *Winnie* with Robert Hardy - was in 1988. Twenty years ago! Hardly a triumphant end to my stage career. The production didn't run more than a few weeks. There were production problems. The American director kept changing his mind. We had to rehearse and put in a new scene that same night on more than one occasion, and the dancers were demoralised having to learn new choreography day by day. I had a couple of songs with Robert and then, one day at rehearsal, the director said he wanted me to sing 'London Pride'. Obviously I was flattered to be asked to sing Noël Coward's famous song, but it was another example of the kind of patchwork quality of the show. Luckily the cast got on well and we were all sorry the parting of the ways came so soon.

From then onwards, as my animal work took up more and more of my time, I couldn't commit myself to months of filming or long runs in the theatre. I mostly took smaller roles in films and worked in television, and, to my delight, I was often asked to take part in poetry readings. Reading poetry is one of my passions and I wish I could do more.

There were, in fact, a couple of highlights for me in the late 1980s and early '90s. The first was a programme called *Sons and Mothers*. Roger Rees and I had worked together in *Hamlet* at Stratford in 1984 and we had so enjoyed 'being' son and mother that we got in touch with a mutual friend, Anne Harvey (whose partner Gervase had been with Bill on the 1993 trip to Cyprus) and asked her if she could devise a programme. I doubt if there is a single poem written that Anne doesn't know about! She put together a wonderful show of excerpts from plays, poetry, songs - even a bit of panto with Aladdin and Widow Twankey - beginning with the birth of the son and ending with the death of the mother. We performed it more times than I can remember and Roger and I sometimes email each other (he lives in New York) to say how wonderful it would be to do it again.

In 1994 Martin Clunes invited me to play a small part in a film he was making called *Staggered*. A brilliantly funny film, it was the story of a young man, kidnapped on his stag night by his best man and 'friends', flown to a remote Scottish island without any clothes on and left to find his way back south! On the island he is met by a dotty old woman collecting firewood (me) who isn't that fazed by his lack of clothing, but lends him a bit of sack and rows him to a nearby island where there is a phone box.

Early on Martin told me that he had seen *Born Free* when he was a boy and how much he had liked it. It was a joy to work with him and the film's producer Philippa (whom he was later to marry), and to start a friendship which developed into Martin becoming a wonderful and very active patron of our charity, The Born Free Foundation.

Another fond memory of this time is playing 'Older Polly' in *The Camomile Lawn*, for which I had to wear brown contact lenses as 'Young Polly', Tara Fitzgerald, had already been cast. (It required an extra half hour in makeup to put the lenses in!) This TV series was directed by Peter Hall, and it is almost impossible to turn down a part if it is offered to you by Peter! I had, in 1963, been invited to play Titania in *A Midsummer Night's Dream* at Stratford, which he was to direct (and also to play Cordelia to Paul Scofield's *King Lear*), but I wasn't very well after the birth of our third child so I was unable to go ahead. Now, thirty-one years later, I was being given a second chance!

IT WASN'T that I didn't enjoy working on the TV play *September* by Rosamunde Pilcher, but it was a bit unreal. Bill had died earlier that year and when I was offered a part I thought it would be good to throw myself into some work. It was, but the film took longer than expected and I felt homesick. What made it special was that one day, going up in the hotel lift, my lift companion asked if I was me! When I told him that I was, he said he was writing a book about a lion and would love me to read it. The man was Michael Morpurgo who, some years later, became the Children's Laureate. When *The Butterfly Lion* was to be recorded he asked me to do it and, later, to record another of his books, *Why the Whales Came*.

Only the other day I heard Michael on the radio, remonstrating about the plan put forward by the government insisting that children as young as three should be taught punctuation. His passionate feelings against this are ones I share. When you are three you need to explore, to experiment, to have adventures in your story-telling. You must be free, not bound by rules. These start soon enough.

Michael is an extraordinary writer. My grandson, Geordie, collects all his books. One, *War Horse*, was made into a massively successful stage play at the National Theatre in 2007. Deeply moving, technically superb, creatively brilliant and wonderfully acted it was, for me, one of the most extraordinary productions I have seen. The 'puppet' horses were flesh and blood, the reality of the First World War conflict tangible. I am in awe of such talent, and I'm not alone. At the performance I attended, the theatre was filled with young people. Their cheers and applause raised the roof.

Many months later I was sitting one afternoon in a packed Olivier Theatre at the National. Onto the stage came a real horse. He was there with his owner and trainer, Kelly Marks. We were all there to meet and listen to Monty Roberts, the world-famous 'Horse Whisperer'. It was, without doubt, one of the most moving experiences I have ever had in the theatre. Monty teaches horses by kindness, by learning their language, by respecting them, by observing their body language. He and George Adamson would have been soulmates. Kelly met him in 1993 and followed his method. We listened to them both and watched Pie, the horse, calmly moving around this totally unfamiliar environment, opposite a huge sea of strange faces.

Then, suddenly, from the back, appeared Joey, one of the 'puppet' horses from the play *War Horse*. Pie, who had seemed so big, all at once looked vulnerable and small. He watched, alert, as Joey, guided by his three handlers walked forward. Ears twitched, feet moved tentatively. The horses eyed, smelled each other.

Joey was a completely 'real' horse! Pie was mesmerised and so were we, watching, holding our breath. And it wasn't a fanciful illusion. Monty told us that when he came to see the play, within the first minute or two he had forgotten he was watching huge puppets designed by Handspring and became totally convinced he was watching live horses.

At the end, when Pie lets Joey greet him, horse-fashion, nuzzling his neck, we were in tears. Oh for a million Monty Roberts. I have his autograph.

Above left: As Rosalind in As You Like It *at the Old Vic, with John Neville as Orlando.*
Above right: With Roger Rees in Sons and Mothers.
Below: With Gary Cooper in The Wreck of the Mary Deare.

OF COURSE we all see people differently. I mentioned earlier about the modesty of actors and perhaps modesty is not a word one might use to describe certain American megastars. But the three I worked with in films were, indeed, kind, generous and modest. In each case I had a 'cameo' role in a major film. The first, *The Wreck of the Mary Deare*, starred the great Gary Cooper. Quiet, unassuming, charming, he dispelled my initial nervousness at working with someone of his calibre. He was, to me, a genuine proponent of 'less is more'. With seemingly so little effort he conveyed so much.

Donald Sutherland was starring in *The Disappearance* and I was asked at very short notice to replace someone. What a chance! Donald was, again, kind, thoughtful and fascinating to talk to. We sat between 'takes' and talked about our families and, as with Gary, I learned so much from watching him.

In *Holocaust 2000* Kirk Douglas was the true action man. I played his wife, who was shot very early on in the story, taking the bullet meant for him! Kirk sensed I was a bit anxious and asked me if I'd like to run through the scene with him quietly before we went on the set. It did the trick.

So for all the hype surrounding American stars, when you meet them they are simply actors, as you are, nervous and determined to get it right, to make the scene work. It doesn't bother me if they have a caravan the size of a palace. That is just how it is, and that can't make you a better actor, can it?

Of course I have my favourite films, television plays and theatre productions. It is impossible to go into them all, but the highlights are taking over from Dorothy Tutin in *The Devils* by John Whiting; playing the wife of Puccini (Robert Stephens) in the TV production directed by Tony Palmer; playing Mrs Darling in the Hallmark TV production of *Peter Pan* starring Danny Kaye and Mia Farrow; a season at the Old Vic which included playing Rosalind in *As You Like It*; playing Juliet on TV opposite Tony Britton with Flora Robson as the nurse (wonderful Dame Flora with whom I had worked in *A Winter's Tale* at the start of my career); and the TV production of *Girls in Uniform* with Francesca Annis, directed by my friend Waris Hussein. These were all very important to me. Some of the parts were very challenging, some made one reveal unexplored emotional depths, all involved working with actors and directors I admired and respected enormously.

Already, however, as the 1980s were ending, so much was changing. Zoo Check was growing, I was writing more and more (articles, poetry, contributing to an occasional book) and leading safaris to Kenya and India. By the year 2000 any stage work was limited to readings, and television appearances and interviews about our animal work (Zoo Check became The Born Free Foundation in 1991).

'Are you an actress', she said.
'Oh...yes'
Part time
Sometime
Hardly ever.
Once, upon a time.

In brave and fearless roles
Fighting the wartime foe
Living with lions
Facing with ever-so British sangfroid
The trials of life.
But now?

All talk of
What shall I wear
Look like
Speak like
Be like
Fade into meaningless mumbo.
Faceless I prefer to remain.
But powerful in spirit
And voice.
Speaking for those that speak not
Fighting for those who are chained
Forced into servitude
Innocent
Helpless.

What is the purpose of life?
We all ask the same.
To do what you can
To be what you are
To care and to love.
With all your immeasurable faults
This is all you can do.

By now I began to feel like a moth emerging from its chrysalis. A new life far from the world of acting. Yet always carrying with me the experiences of the past, valuing old friendships, treasuring new ones, with eyes wide open and an eagerness to learn. Feeling a deep gratitude that this new life had given me a chance to immerse myself in a cause about which Bill and Will and I felt so strongly.

They say that the eyes are the windows of the soul. If that is true, the eyes of all the imprisoned animals I have seen burn deep into mine. I have never understood why so many people believe that animals have no souls. Perhaps replace that word with *spirit*: for me they are interchangeable. It is about the intangible, the indescribable, the invisible essence of a being whether they are living or dead, human or animal. Sometimes these spirits return to reproach us, sometimes to comfort us, sometimes to reassure us we are not alone.

Whether in Japan, China, Thailand, France, Britain, America, India, it makes no difference, the eyes of the thousands of animals I've seen are with me. I have seen their hopelessness, bewilderment, resignation, frustration, and I have deliberately turned all these negative memories into positive thought. Of course, huge numbers of these animals are now dead – I'm talking about the past 40 years or so. But that isn't the point. Their eyes light this rocky, treacherous path we had chosen to tread.

Don't others see these eyes? If they do, why can't they read their message? They see the look in the eyes of their own pets, but there it stops. The tiger, the snow leopard, the caged parrot, the squirrel monkey and the elephants killed for their ivory, all ignored. As George Adamson used to say, to really understand animals you have to get 'behind their eyes'. Perhaps some people are afraid to do that, the message would be too disturbing. Perhaps today, when we place so much emphasis on face value – what we look like, what we wear, the 'image' – we have little time to spare to look below the surface.

It is true to say that some zoos have made improvements over the past few years. Larger enclosures, more stimulating environments. But! One might say the Dorchester Hotel is really comfortable, great food, warm in winter and all the rest. But if you could never leave it, would you feel the same? Personally speaking, if I could never choose my own companions, or if I had none, or could not choose what time I got up or went to bed, how long would it be before I went crazy? Not all captive animals become disturbed, but many do. The signs are obvious: swaying, head-weaving, over-grooming all reveal 'stereo-typic' behaviour. And sustaining this commercial wildlife 'business' is the so-called 'right' of us humans to view everything that moves and breathes.

On the back cover of *Island Visitor*, the guide to the Isle of Wight, the broadcaster and naturalist Chris Packham is quoted as saying 'If I was a tiger I'd know where I'd want to be - fabulous new enclosures and the best of care'. He would rather be in captivity than in the wild. How strange.

I have never seen a tiger in the wild 'burning bright in the forests of the night', but I have had the privilege of visiting a reserve they inhabit, and have seen their footprints. For me it is enough to know they are there. Thank heavens there are millions of people trying desperately to protect the wild tigers that remain. Trying to save their habitat. Ensuring that India's symbol does not end up only as a photo in a book, or a shadow of itself in a zoo.

Many years ago, in Scotland, an elderly man in a pub and I got into conversation. 'What do you believe in?' he said. 'Nature', I replied. I did not need to reflect. I just knew. And still do.

What is nature? There is a great deal of talk and endeavour to protect nature, the animals, the birds, the whales and dolphins, to clean the polluted rivers, the lakes, the green fields, and so on. Nature is not put together by thought, as religion is, as belief is. Nature is the tiger, that extraordinary animal with its energy, its great sense of power. Nature is the solitary tree in the field, the meadows and the grove; it is that squirrel shyly hiding behind a bough. Nature is the ant and the bee and all the living things of the earth. Nature is the river, not a particular river, whether the Ganges, the Thames, or the Mississippi. Nature is all those mountains, snowclad with the dark blue valleys and range of hills meeting the sea…one must have a feeling for all this, not destroy it, not kill for one's pleasure.

J Krishnamurti, November 1983

J Krishnamurti, an extraordinary, profound, humble man was a close friend of my daughter Louise's godmother, Mary Zimbalist (widow of Sam who produced the film *Ben Hur*). She travelled with him and looked after him until his death. And she brought him to our home when Christian, the lion, was living here in 1970. From what I have been told he always remembered seeing that gorgeous golden creature. For my part, I always remember J Krishnamurti, hearing him speak, opening up minds, breaking down preconceptions and barriers. He understood about animals. He would have understood George.

We travelled to J Krishnamurti's homeland in 1986, taking with us six tigers that had been confiscated from a tawdry little circus by Maidstone Council. Confiscated because they didn't have the right paperwork, not because the six animals were stuffed together in one beast wagon! So much for animal welfare laws in the 1980s.

Bill and I had gone to Karnataka State, in India, before we did our trek in Zanskar, at the invitation of the then Chief Minister, Mr Hegde, introduced to us by our producer Rani Dube. I had met him and told him about the Cross Brothers Circus tigers and how we were hoping to rehome them in a sanctuary in India. 'I'll show you where you could make a place for them,' he said.

The vast area of trees and shrubs was like heaven compared to their wretched wagon. Just a few months later we had raised enough funds through an appeal with *The Mail on Sunday* to fly the tigers, with vet and assistants, to their new life. School children joined us and Mr Hegde at the Sanctuary where, after a blessing by a holy man, the animals took their first steps on earth, felt the breeze, stared in amazement at the butterflies and tentatively explored their new-found paradise. It was the first animal rescue we had done and we felt very moved, and relieved all had gone well. One of the tigers, named Greenwich, the survivor of the group, died as recently as 2007. He was moved up to a new Sanctuary we had made in a different part of the Park for another six tigers we had brought from the Big Cat Sanctuary in Kent. You really could say he died of old age. And at peace.

The 'Laws' of Nature

THEY SAY THAT WRITING is a lonely business. And it is true in one way. Now and again I do see kind friends. But Bill and I never led a very social life and, I suppose, in that way, nothing has changed. But I do miss interesting conversations with men! I have some close and dear women friends – some I have known, it seems, forever. But Bill was a man of many and fascinating experiences and was such an interesting person to sit and talk with. A man's perspective on the world is different, and I still have a thirst for that kind of conversation. I am constantly reminded of how little I know, and how little I remember! Old age! Not that I mind growing old. We arrive at threescore years and ten and a bit beyond if we're lucky. Like tiger Greenwich, happy to sleep and eat and then drift away. What a tiny pinprick of difference each of us makes in the world, this heart-stoppingly beautiful world we seem to be shattering and crumbling and changing. When the hurricanes hurl their force, the floods submerge the earth, the droughts burn all to dust, I think nature is ringing bells. Look. Listen. Stop. In the end nature will adapt and change. Can we?

Sometimes it is lonely but sometimes it is crazily crowded. As I look at my collection of notebooks – an essential part of my travels – the faces of the animals rush towards me. Silent. But I understand all too well what they are telling me. And what have they done wrong? Nothing.

Fear of the hare as it runs for its life
Fear of the lamb as it faces the knife
Fear of the bird as it's trapped in its cage
Fear of the dog of its master's rage.

Fear of the fox as it hears 'tally ho'
Fear of the whale as the harpoon strikes low
Fear of the wolf as it flees from the gun
Fear of the bear as it 'dances' for fun

Fear of the badger dug out of its lair
Fear of the animal caught in a snare
Fear of the elephant as poachers give chase
Fear of all creatures when dangers they face.

Fear for ourselves. When the reckoning comes.

Bill had a very favourite quotation by American naturalist Henry Beston, who died in 1968 and was one of the founders of the modern environmental movement. And it has become mine as well.

> For the animal shall not be measured by man. In a world older and more complete than ours, they move finished and complete, gifted with extensions of the senses we have lost or never attained, living by voices we shall never hear. They are not brethren; they are not underlings; they are other nations, caught with ourselves in the net of life and time, fellow prisoners of the splendour and travail of the earth.
>
> *Henry Beston, 'The Outermost House'*

There is an endless list of great thinkers and writers who speak about compassion and understanding, who implore us not to use animals as 'merchandise', to be bought and sold – alive or as 'body parts' – to be hunted for fun, for trophies. As Albert Schweitzer said, 'Until he extends the circle of his compassion to all living things, man will not himself find peace. ' And we haven't, have we?

Almost everyone experiences a moment when their life changes in some way. Sometimes so unobtrusively it is barely noticed. It could be something they read, someone they meet, someone who inspires them. 'A robin redbreast in a cage / Puts all heaven in a rage' isn't just a fragment of a famous poem by Blake. It entreats us to search our conscience, our heart. I never met Elsa the lioness but her spirit led me to where I stand today. My feelings about the natural world. For me, it's not just the 'Big Five' (I deeply dislike this term, which assumes the pre-eminence of lion, leopard, elephant, buffalo and rhino), nor the bears and the antelope, the charismatic species. It is the fullness of nature. Bugs and bees, forests and flowers, ocean and river life and birds on the wing. The balance of nature on earth is infinitely complex and interwoven and few people stand back and observe, or try to understand. Nature might as well be wallpaper!

Joy Adamson with the famous Elsa.

Others stride in with their saws and guns and snares and sense of superiority. Or make laws, sitting behind great desks, about what it is OK to kill or trade, and what we could allow to live a bit longer. Our arrogance is immeasurable.

In my mind's eye – bird's eye –
I see the African plains.
Dry, huge, far as the eye of whatever kind
Can see.

Mountains on the edge of the sky
Stand violet, and inviolate.
Sentinels stretching to clouds.
Clouds forever changing the space pattern of blue.

Thornbush, acacia,
Umbrella pools of sanctuary and shade
In noon-day fire.
Grey coolness harbouring grey majesty
Of elephants.
Nature's monarchs.
Nature's great teachers.

Trunks curling and caressing,
Ears giant palm leaves,
Fanning,
To cool the noon-hot blood.
Wise eyes, lash-curtained,
High forehead. Noble.
Harbouring an ancient store of memories.

Flash of ivory amongst the grey.
Ivory-coloured prizes.
Coveted for carvings.
Unthroning mammoth kings and queens alike.
Returning all to dust.

My mind's eye weeps for you
As you fall to earth.
My small heart bleeds for yours
As your blood is spilled.

Red blood, splattering the earth
And thirst-racked thorns.
Scarlet on ivory –
Momentarily.
Then snatched away to light some vaulted store.
The ivory gleam has gone.
And darkness comes again to Africa.

I wish these decision-makers could have walked with us on the dawn-lit plains in Kenya, in 1964, with George and a couple of lions for company. The tall grasses, threaded with dew-damp cobwebs, shining in the pale sun. The smell of honey from the lions' wet fur leading us on to explore the still silent morning world. Sadly there are few

'George Adamsons' left, watching and learning, understanding and loving, with no strings attached.

Many, many years ago I was invited by an old friend, Betty Darrell-Smith, to go to Halifax, Nova Scotia, to see the newborn seals on the ice. My youngest son, Dan, came with us. It was a strange and somewhat unsettling experience.

We flew in a helicopter to the Madeleine Islands where this encounter was to take place. Beforehand we were given a talk about what we could and couldn't do. I already had mixed feelings as I knew that the pristine creamy-white coat of the pups and their liquid brown eyes do not make them immune from the cull, the brutal clubbing. Even after a few weeks, when the coat has lost its snowflake purity, the young pup is still vulnerable because of its prized haircoat and oil. Yes, there are millions of seals, but what kind of person beats a baby to death?

We landed on the ice, with strict instructions not to go too close to the young or to touch them. One of the first things I saw was an American lady manoeuvering her way on her tummy towards a pup. She stopped only a couple of feet away and took her picture. Yes, *she* was making the rules. The little one's eyes seemed to open a little wider but it didn't move. I wish I could have read its mind.

It was a breathtakingly beautiful environment. Sparkling. Sharp air that cleansed you through and through. I drank it all in, but I felt a deep sadness. That, I suppose, is as it always will be. Nature and how we treat it.

The Family Trees

YESTERDAY, VERY EARLY, I walked in the woods. It was still, calm, damp-smelling after the night's rain. The paths were moss-cushioned, the trees a tangle of branches and species and shapes. Yes, perhaps coppicing is something to think about. So hard to think of change! I love things as they are, even old and crumbling. When the children were small Bill and I sometimes thought we would move the sitting room furniture around a bit. Not a popular idea! 'We liked it as it was!' rose the cry.

So, yes, coppicing would let in more light, encourage more wild flowers, create a more varied habitat. I am thinking about it! But, this particular morning I had an urge to visit the huge ancient beech tree, with its long, enticing, to-be-balanced-on arms heavily leaning on the leaf-thick ground. Here was an old familiar friend; here all was the same. I touched the lovely silvery grey-green trunk and thanked Mother Nature for leaving this treasure when the hurricane of 1987 toppled almost all the others.

Trees of all kinds are a life force. Family trees as well. Who knows how far back we can trace our characteristics and behaviour patterns? My great-grandfather, William Columban McKenna, was described in a biography by my great-uncle, author Stephen McKenna, as an 'impetuous iconoclast from County Monaghan', whose creed was that 'individuals should be free to work out their own salvation, to shape their own destiny.' (Dr Robert Colley's article in the *Clann MacKenna Journal* No 7.) A man after my own heart. His son, Reginald, of Chancellor of the Exchequer and Chairman of the Midland Bank fame, was a realist, a private person – following Disraeli's principle: 'Never complain, Never explain'.

From my grandmother Ethel Mackenzie's tree descended more artistic branches. Actors Charles Mackenzie (who performed as Henry Compton), Herbert Beerbohm Tree, Fay Compton, author Compton Mackenzie, Edward Compton and, much further down, through the marriage of Jean Compton to Arthur Howard, Alan Howard, with whom I had the great pleasure of working a few months ago at the Queen Elizabeth Hall, as readers with the 'The Sixteen' choir, in two concerts of choral music entwined with the spoken word - by Poulenc, Brecht, Monteverdi and Auden, to name a few. I wish I had known this when we met!

But the direct upward branch from my father, Terence, introduced other elements and skills. His great-great-grandfather was Stephen Mackenzie, the physician, who lectured in pathology and clinical medicine, was a physician at Moorfield's Eye Hospital and was knighted in the year of his death in 1909. His great-grandfather was Sir Morell Mackenzie, who operated on the Prussian Crown Prince (later Emperor) Frederick. No more medical talents seem to have emerged since then and it is the more creative genes that appear to have taken over. Certainly when combined with the musical gifts of my mother and her siblings, so happily passed down to our children and grandchildren, it would seem that, generally speaking, the heart rules the head. I'm not sure that is always a good thing! Our grandchildren no doubt will prove me wrong!

I was intrigued to discover, many years ago, that the McKenna shield depicts a hunting scene. Somewhere down the line that particular aspect of my inherited interests has been turned on its head! By the time it reached me it certainly had!

All those intriguing ancestors that I never knew. Although I met Compton Mackenzie once - and Fay Compton, as I have said, when my father took me to see her in a play - I didn't know them and, having no first cousins on my father's side, there was no one of my age to keep the family connection alive. When my stepmother, Gladys, died in July 1996 it really brought that chapter to a close. My poor father, with whom so much had prevented me becoming close, had been greatly loved by her. But it seemed his dashing good looks and attractive personality had been no match for the ill health which dogged his life and, I guess, the somewhat difficult temperament that coloured his relationships.

Even as a young man, a lieutenant in The 8th Kings Royal Irish Hussars at the start of the First World War, he was constantly on 'sick leave'. His severe abdominal problems leading to an operation and the authorities declaring him unfit to return to active service in France. Finally, in 1918 he was declared permanently unfit and left the services. One can only imagine how disappointed he must have felt, how demoralised. His self-esteem and confidence deeply damaged. 'Permanently' is a heavy millstone to carry.

His first marriage in 1926 was to Joyce Philipson (whose daughter, Jennifer, by a second marriage I have had the great good fortune to meet!). His best man was Harry Tennent, of H M Tennent no less, the famous theatre production company which gave me my first job in London in 1950, twenty-four years later! How strangely everything is linked.

I am not quite sure where he met my mother, but I imagine it must have been romantic and exciting – both of them with strong personalities and extremely attractive. But my father's financial circumstances hit hard times and everything changed. When I was born we lived in York Terrace, by Regent's Park – one of those elegant, tall cream houses with cascades of stairs. My room was right at the top with Nanny, and I was brought down at teatime to see my parents. How remote and strange that sounds. But, of course, I knew nothing else, and when the 'crash' came I was four, and fortunes changed beyond recognition. Later, my mother told me she had to sell all her jewellery, and then the door was closed on York Terrace, and on my parents' marriage. I moved with my father to Hampstead: Fourteen Fellowes Road, a maisonette. My mother moved to a flat off the Strand, and I visited her sometimes at weekends. It was very difficult for everyone. I remember crying at the bus stop when I had to say goodbye to Nanny, and can only imagine my mother's feelings.

At Daddy's we had lots of animals. Cats, dogs, budgies, a grass snake called George, a parrot (who bit everyone except my father) and two bush babies. To think of it now my heart sinks! But this was 1935. I didn't know then what I know now.

I was very strictly brought up. Good manners at table, straight back, no answering back. Once, on a walk with Nanny, I thought I'd be really clever and race home first. My triumphant smile as I greeted her at our gate soon turned to tears as I was given a good slap bottom and sent to bed with no tea. Nanny had been terrified I was lost. I understood that later. There are so many things we carry with us from childhood. There was a day when I broke a cup washing up and Bill found me in tears. 'It's only a cup,' he said; 'a 'thing. It was an accident.' He was so comforting, and gradually I learned to deal with the memories of the accidents I had had as a child and for which I had been punished. I have never been cross with my own children when they broke something by mistake.

Our life in Fellowes Road ended in 1938 when we moved to Slinfold in Sussex and I attended weekly boarding school in Horsham. I was to say goodbye to my dear Nanny, the constant companion of my seven year lifetime but to my great joy Phyllis, my father's housekeeper, was coming with us.

In recent years I have driven through Slinfold in a vain search for our old home, but it has all changed so much. I drove in and around the village without success. I remember it was a comfortable house with a lovely garden. I would ride my bike and live out my imaginary stories with my imaginary friends to my heart's content. In winter the pond froze over. Daddy brought a gramophone down and I attempted to skate to the music without falling over too often. His favourite song was Stephen Foster's 'I Dream of Jeannie with the Light Brown Hair'. (He always used to sing 'I Dream of *Ginny*…'.)

When, one day, he said he wanted to talk to me about something, I was completely unprepared for the bombshell he was about to drop. Real bombshells had been falling on London and he had decided he wanted me to go to a place of safety. South Africa, with my mother. I don't think I said very much. I was used to dealing with things quietly and privately. I was sitting on the floor by his knees and he put his arms around me.

I have felt so sad, writing about the memories of my father. His figure at the station, waving goodbye as my mother and I travelled to Liverpool to catch the boat to Cape Town. I can never again put my arms around him.

His younger brother Justin (after whom our second son was named) was killed in the First World War. He was twenty-one. Like my father, he went to Oxford University and, like him, he joined the forces when war broke out, in his case The Kings Royal Rifle Corps. However, in 1917 he transferred to the Royal Flying Corps. This Corps was unfortunately also known as the 'suicide club' and Justin had only been flying for thirty-nine days when he was shot down over France and killed. He is buried at the Cabaret-Rouge British Cemetery at Souchez in the Pas de Calais. He was such a beautiful looking young man.

My uncle Gerald (who served in the Navy) I saw little of, although, after his death, I used to visit Aunt Emily, his widow, who lived at Kirtling Tower in Newmarket. Once Bill and I took the children there and we camped in the garden. It is thanks to Aunt Emily that I have Morell Mackenzie's silver punch-bowl. A true family heirloom.

My family

Above left: My father during World War I.

Above right: His wedding to my stepmother Gladys.

Right: My mother's sister Marguerite.

Far right, top and bottom: Studies of my mother's brother Uncle Peter.

Below: Uncle Peter with Marguerite's son, my cousin Johnny.

Virginia McKenna

Bill's family

Far left: His grandfather Lindon Travers.

Left: His father's sister Daisy Linda Ward.

Below: His three sisters, Linden (left), Pearl (middle) and Alice (right).

Bottom: His brother Ken and Ken's wife Gemma.

Louise in her teens

I MISS MY daughter Louise very much although, in a strange way, the yearly visits I make to see her family in Australia bind us together in a very particular fashion. She is a fiercely protective mother and a strong person. She has had to be. It isn't easy to hold your head high, pursue your job as a piano and singing teacher and be so far from the close support system your family can bring you. Her personal relationships haven't lasted and, occasionally, have been traumatic, but from them she has four lovely children.

My granddaughters, Ashlin and Tess, are hugely musical: both violinists, although Tess seems to play anything she puts her hand to – piano, saxophone, drums! What will be next! Ashlin is a fine performer with a rich warm tone. But I think her other talent is as a teacher and already, at 20 years old, she has several students. She lives an independent life with her boyfriend Chris, but nothing can break the closeness she has to her mother.

My eldest grandson, Lindon, is the intellectual. A person with a deep sense of responsibility. He has just added another dimension to that with the birth of his little son, Alex, in January 2008. He and his partner, Aliesha, are devoted to each other and, knowing Lindon, he will somehow be able to juggle parenthood with his university studies. Law and philosophy are his subjects.

Geordie, at 15, is an extremely interesting boy. Vulnerable, sensitive, fun, immersed in martial arts, developing a real talent for writing and now music. He and I have a great time playing poker when I visit (having been led down that slippery slope by Vincent Ball, an old actor friend from *A Town Like Alice* days. He came and stayed last time I was in Australia and we were to have endless poker sessions, to Geordie's delight).

I keep having these enchanting, visual memories of Louise as a little girl – unquenchable tomboy

Tess, Alex, Louise and Ashlin

as she 'kept up' with her brothers – gorgeous, wilful teenager, a graceful dancer, enthusiastic gymnast, talented piano player – rebellious schoolgirl!

She is still beautiful now, but that young girl with long flaxen hair was breathtaking. Determined too. Aged seven, she was the first in our family to become a vegetarian – then a vegan – then a fruitarian. This lasted only a few months as her energy began to fade!

Lindon, Aliesha, Alex, Ashlin, Chris, Geordie, Tess

In our family emotions run deep but are kept quite private. I respect that. As a woman I suppose I am more likely to express my feelings, but I try not to burden people with them. And that goes for our daughter, Louise, as well – now a grandmother! At last a role that will, I hope, bring her nothing but joy. She writes and talks glowingly about little Alexander William and every few weeks drives the five hours to Perth to see him when Lindon can't bring them south. Although, or perhaps because, she is on her own now I know she is much happier. I just wish she could see her brothers more and that the children could get to know each other. But you have to accept what you can't change.

Louise as a child in Sardinia

WILL'S DAUGHTER, LILY, and son William (Wij) are talented. Lily is beautiful, artistic and an untrained but instinctively gifted actress and has already been shortlisted for three major films. One day I know she will be chosen. Although her mother Carrie and Will have parted they remain friends and I admire Carrie for the way she has dealt with her changed life. Her mother Anne and her stepfather Terry have always been very kind to our family. Terry, in fact, was a Trustee of Born Free for several years.

Will as a baby, with his father

Will, who rarely reveals personal difficulties, has thrown himself completely into his work for the Born Free Foundation, to a degree that is remarkable and, for me, deeply touching. Sometimes his physical resemblance to Bill is heartstopping. And he, like his father, is a man of vision and a leader.

Wij is a 'one-off'. Enormously bright, deeply affectionate, sport-mad, he is a real ray of sunshine. I'm hoping he will be Prime Minister! Brilliant at maths and science, English, languages, sport and cares about people. What more could one want!

Will

Wij

Lily

Virginia McKenna

JUSTIN AND CHARLOTTE'S pair, Jack and little Emily, are adorable. They all lived with me for nine months when their house was being extended, and so I shared their lives in a very special way. Jack is sensitive and vulnerable, with emotions near the surface. He is a great companion and I love it when he stays the night.

Jack

Emily is huge fun, very articulate, a strong personality and very loving. My daughter-in-law Charlotte, a former paediatric nurse, is exceptionally thoughtful as a person and has been really generous in fostering a close relationship between the children and myself. I think she realises what that means to me.

Justin has been a tower of strength. When Bill died both he and Dan came back to live with me for quite a long time – Justin for about a year, and Dan for longer. Justin continues to be my rock in matters

Emily

of finance, about which I know little and which Bill always dealt with. Without Justin I would have truly floundered.

Justin and Charlotte

He, too, is in the film business, as a first assistant director. When he was young both he and Will worked with Bill on his documentaries, so there is little he doesn't understand about 'the business'. I had the greatest joy working with him on a short film, written and directed by Amanda Waring, the late Dorothy Tutin's daughter. I watched him working quietly, making sure things were in place, on time, sometimes offering a suggestion, always sensitive to the actors and the mood of the scene. I felt very proud.

Luca (right) with his cousin Jack

Dan as a boy

LITTLE FOUR-YEAR OLD Luca is the son of my son Dan and his partner Adnana. Luca is devoted to his parents, but I am happy he and I have a friendly, fun relationship. He likes to spend hours enacting games of pirates and divers, delving into a 'dressing-up' chest to produce an array of costumes from Power Ranger, to pirate, to Batman, to a Halloween skeleton. He is very good at building complicated Lego structures. So Dan, who is a brilliant DIY man, has, I believe, a live-in assistant!

Dan and Adnana both work. She is a lovely girl – a model, who uses her swimming skills to work underwater. Dan started his working life as a model (though he qualified as a graphic artist), but then trained as a diver. He has worked on many commercials and films as the 'safety guy' underwater, teaching and monitoring the actors or models who are working in front of the camera , as well as building sets and installing the electrics. He has done some work in front of the camera but not enough in my view. He is a good-looking boy!

Both he and Adnana work whenever the opportunity presents itself. Like most young couples, they can't afford not to. Especially now as I have been told the exciting news that another baby is expected. Dan is tender-hearted and conscientious, always thoughtful and kind.

Sara and Jessie

Laying flowers at Bill's grave

ALTHOUGH SHE IS not my daughter, my step-daughter Anna is someone I hold dear to my heart. I have known her since she was three and we have always been friends. She shared a lot of our life, coming on holidays, visiting us in Kenya in 1964, holding her wedding reception at our house, becoming a close friend of Louise. She and her Canadian husband Carl had two daughters, Sara and Jessie, and made their home in Toronto. A lot of water has flowed under the bridge since then.

Sadly, Anna and Carl parted; they 'shared' the children and it was a well thought-through arrangement. The girls seemed comfortable and happy. One morning, when Anna was staying with us, I was washing up in the kitchen and she told me that over the years she had known something was different in her. She liked women, not men. She was a lesbian. I knew how hard it was for her to tell me. Gay rights were not even whispered about then, but I was so happy she had confided in me. Her coming out made not one bit of difference to me. I loved the person she was, and still do. The most important thing, I knew, was that she should talk to Bill direct. He mustn't hear it from anyone else.

'Go for a walk in the woods with him'. They did. I sensed it would be hard for him but, as in all major issues, he was understanding, accepting. Anna has been in a very long-term relationship with an extremely nice woman, Bev. Wonderful Bev who, when Bill died and they came over from Canada, took over the kitchen and kept us going with soups and homely meals, at a time when food was the last thing on our minds.

Bev and Anna

I asked Anna if I could touch on her story in this book and she said I could. In a way, it epitomises what I feel. I have several gay friends and they are some of the kindest, most loyal people one could ever meet. And who are we to 'judge' anyway? There are too many no-go areas, too many rules, prejudices, discriminations, busy-bodies! Real love is a blessing and should be blessed.

The fascinating thing to me is that my father's and mother's families are joined not only by marriage but by a little seaside town. Etretat! The Irish/Scottish McKennas and the French/Scottish Dennis would have known each other in earlier days as my father's aunt, Aggie, had a villa there and so my darling GrinGran, my mother, aunt and uncles would have met and mingled with each other. My great-aunt Aggie had a stone seat erected on the cliff by the chapel in memory of great-uncle Ernest (Reginald's brother). It was destroyed by the Germans. How pointless.

So, now, of close family there is little left on my father's or mother's side. Some cousins whom I rarely see except at funerals. Only my first cousin Johnny, his former wife, Doris, and their children remain in my life. And my Uncle John's widow, Colette. She and I are in regular communication and I treasure her friendship and her interest in my little family. Uncle John was only thirteen when his father died and, according to family stories, a bit unruly! So he was sent to Winchester (Uncle Peter had already left) and suffered a number of beatings – one for forgetting to put on his slippers! Sadly, when the family money was lost he had to leave school. He returned to Le Havre, into the cotton business for a while, followed by military service in the French Cavalry. But then GrinGran suggested he write to the Director of Source Perrier, whom she knew, and there – apart from the Second World War – he remained until he retired, rising to the position of Director. In the war he served in the French Cavalry and ended up in Germany as liaison officer with the British and French governments, tracing French prisoners of war. He was a fine, tall man, his striking looks strangely enhanced by his prominent nose which he had broken in a motorbike accident when he was young!

A lover of golf and bridge, he and Colette sadly had no children but lived happily with and for each other. Then illness, hospitals, clinics, nurses. Then death. Colette needed the strength she is well-known for. Now she has my cousin's family, our family and her friends.

For John and Colette

C'est comme tu dormais
Le front sans rides
Les mains calmes.
Je touche la joue

Je t'embrasse
Mes lèvres chaudes
Sur ta peau fraîche
Où es-tu?
Ton corps n'est plus
L'abri de ton âme –
Elle vole au ciel
Elle court parmi les étoiles
Elle nous entoure,
Avec une bague de tendresse.
Elle est partout.
Ne t'éloignes pas trop.
Tiens la main de Colette
Qui a tenu la tienne,
Avec une telle dévotion
C'est dur effacer
Dans un instant
Les liens d'une vie.

Quant à nous
Ta famille
Tu ne changeras jamais
Cet oncle si beau
Charmant, aimable.
Un gentilhomme suranné.
Merci pour ton amitié
Et merci à Dieu
Pour ta vie.

My mother's siblings were all very special, all very different. My other uncle, Peter, was the non-conformist. He had attended Winchester as a boy but was forced to leave through ill health. He was a wonderful pianist – and taught both piano and English in Paris where he lived (and he actually *made* a radio!). He lived so frugally and modestly. We were never allowed to visit him in his pint-sized flat, but when we finally persuaded him in his latter years to move south to Nîmes, where he could be near John and Colette, his things had to be packed up and the flat closed. I know that was a sad experience for his brother and Colette. He obviously had spent nothing on himself.

We all adored Uncle Peter and when, eventually, it became impossible for him to travel any more, the Christmases and summers never felt the same. I used to go to Nîmes and visit him as often as I could. I would wheel him in his wheelchair out into the garden of the nursing home, and we would sit and talk for hours about the family and the past. Dan loved him too and he and Adnana went to see him, for what turned out to be the last time. Adnana took some very poignant black and white photographs of him. She had them framed and they hang in my bedroom so I can say 'Bonjour' each day to this still-missed uncle.

When he died, Will and I went to Nîmes for the funeral. Afterwards we returned to the nursing home to sort out his few possessions. They were contained in three black plastic bags. And I thought that put everything in perspective. Sad though it was to see how little Uncle Peter possessed, I knew that, for him, life was nothing to do with what you have. It is what you are, what you give of yourself that matters. It is your love for your family that you hold more precious than any possession – and he certainly had all of ours.

My aunt Marguerite was Uncle Peter's rock. He visited her for lunch nearly every Sunday and she kept an eye on him. I was always conscious of how elegant 'Maggie' was. As Directrice of Molyneux in Paris I suppose it was part of her style and personality. But whatever she wore, however simple, she always looked chic and marvellous. My mother and I seemed to dress in a more haphazard way, but Maggie was different. She and Johnny's father, Henry de Buys Roessingh, divorced when Johnny was young and she never remarried. She was a good friend to me and, looking back, I know how lucky I was to have a few wise family members to turn to if I needed to talk through problems – or let off steam!

And my luck continued as, in the mid-1950s, into the vacuum that they say nature abhors, poured the huge Travers tribe. The in-laws, cousins, aunties, uncles, nieces and nephews, the vast tree continuously sprouting a bewildering number of leaf-laden branches. For me, it was a dream come true.

Generous, spirited, warm, and beautiful, Bill's sisters, Linden, Pearl and Alice were stunning, and talented as well. Lin was a very well-known actress, having worked in Alfred Hitchcock's film *The Lady Vanishes*, and numerous other films including her favourite, *No Orchids for Miss Blandish*. Her acting talent was inherited by her eldest daughter, Suzy, who married Cornel Lucas, the famous and delightful photographer. I first met 'Corny' at Pinewood Studios in the 1950s when I was under contract to J Arthur Rank, and he was the Studio's stills photographer. I am lucky enough to have many of his pictures of both Bill and myself and they evoke memories that stretch back to a past I treasure.

Lin's daughter Sally, by her second marriage to Jim Holman (of the famous engineering and mining equipment company Holman Brothers in Camborne, Cornwall), inherited her mother's other talent as an artist. That artist streak appeared in so many of Bill's family and he was deeply proud of his Aunt Daisy, his father's sister, who in middle age created still-life paintings which are part of the Daisy Linda Ward collection in the Ashmolean Museum in Oxford.

In 2008 I went with my son Dan to Oxford to visit Aunt Daisy's collection in the Ashmolean Museum. It was a very special and privileged experience, as the Museum was closed that day and we were given a private tour, thanks to the kindness of Jon Whiteley, Senior Assistant Keeper in the Department of Western Art.

We followed him up and down stairways, along galleries, through locked doors and, finally, came to 'the room'. As the door opened a blaze of beauty and colour greeted us. A collection of 17th-century Dutch and Flemish 'still life' paintings covered the walls. Flowers, fruit, sea creatures, birds – each painting was extraordinary in its own way. Some were large, some miniature. In each the detail, the lustre, the reflection of light created an illusion of 'living life'. Dan and I were entranced. Two of Aunt Daisy's own paintings hung with the collection, both of great beauty and completely in the style of the rest. It was on her death that Theodore, her husband, had bequeathed 94 works from their collection to the Museum.

Some of the other paintings had recently come up for sale and I decided to buy two small ones to keep Aunt Daisy in the family, which I know is what Bill would have wanted. She, too, was musical and a performer, appearing in Puccini's *Manon Lescaut* at Covent Garden and the lead in *The Mikado*. Her sister, Alice, was an excellent pianist who accompanied top artists John McCormack and Marie Hall.

I have been trying to trace the origins of this wealth of talent and although, no doubt, others may discover even earlier beginnings, I believe it all started with Lindon Travers, who was born in 1850 in Halifax. He was the son of a Wesleyan minister, who accompanied

Wilberforce to Jamaica and supported his efforts to bring about the abolition of slavery. I know Bill was very moved by that. (We have just marked, in 2007, the Bicentenary of the Abolition of the Slave Trade Act.)

However, it emerged that Lindon had an exceptionally fine bass singing voice and he was invited to perform on stage. This was 'contrary to Wesleyan ideas in the Victorian era' – according to my late father-in-law, and so Lindon changed his name. First to Kenneth Lindon and, subsequently, to Lindon Travers (by deed poll).

Lindon left his job of school headmaster and embarked on a fascinating career in 'Show Business'. Apart from the concerts, he became a presenter and narrator for both musical and educational shows. 'Around the World in 120 Minutes!' was a ground-breaker – the earliest form of 'Picture Entertainment'. This eventually developed into the slide picture show and Lindon built up a popular series of educational lectures, tracing his travels in Europe and to South Africa, which culminated in his Fellowship of the Royal Geographical Society, an honour my son Will also has over a hundred years later.

How times have changed. Being 'on stage' 150 years ago was deeply frowned on. Now acting is applauded and admired as a profession and, following the thespian thread through the Travers family, it is thrilling to see the tradition so brilliantly upheld by Bill's niece, Penelope Wilton (one of our country's finest actresses), Charlotte Lucas (Suzy's daughter) and, until recently, Pearl's daughter Angela Morant and her brother Richard.

Being a part of Bill's family, I forgot I was an only child. Bill's sisters and my brother-in-law Ken's wife, Gemma, were close and very important friends. Alice (Penelope's mother), who died tragically young, of cancer, was one of the most adorable people you could ever meet. Her hair had turned white in her twenties and framed this smiling, lovely face with its huge dark eyes. She was Louise's second godmother and brought light and fun into all our lives.

I think about all these people I knew, and did not know, about their final resting places or whether their ashes were scattered on the breeze. Bill and my mother lie in graves next to each other in my village. Uncle Peter's ashes are scattered in our garden and the woods. We still belong to each other.

The Spirit of Elsa

I HAVE A SECOND FAMILY too. A family that also supports me, that I can turn to, to which I owe so much, a growing family with many of whom I have travelled the past quarter of a century. My Born Free family. Elsa, the lioness, is the true mother of this family. We are her children, her descendants, her messengers, carrying her story and her spirit with us into people's minds and hearts. Or trying to. Some people welcome us. Some are confused. Others stare, uncomprehending. Others show their contempt. Or laugh. It is of no consequence. When Bill and I went to Kenya to film the *Born Free* story it became, without us knowing it, the rest-of-our-life story. *Born Free* is the second film that is still a part of me.

We began our two month 'getting-to-know-you' period with the ex-circus lionesses chosen to play the part of Elsa by going into an enclosure with the young German trainer, Monika. One of the lionesses, Astra, was waiting. We were given leather wrist guards to wear as a protection from the possibility of a paw swipe, which might tear one of our veins. We were also given two short sticks and taught to position them in certain ways: crossed, turned sideways, signals the animals would recognise. I recall Monika putting a piece of meat on the end of one of the sticks. Astra rose to her feet from where she had been lying on a low platform. She looked enormous. Her brow was heavy. Her movements slow, deliberate. I knew I was the one being trained now! When I came out of the enclosure I was trembling a little. Someone gave me a cup of tea. People laughed. Tension eased. I longed to get back to the children. Our real world.

The days passed and our training continued. 'Yes, you can touch her now/stroke her now/let her come up to you now...' until the morning Bill went into the compound with Monika and Astra was in a very different frame of mind. Something had upset her and she was far from welcoming. Bill was in her sights. Monika managed to get between him and Astra and Bill got out as quietly and slowly as he could. The two producers, Tom McGowan (the original director, who left and was replaced by James Hill) and George were watching. As was I.

The following day Astra behaved similarly towards George and, again, towards Bill. It was a defining moment. Astra and Djuba were immediately withdrawn from close contact work. And then there were none. The search began. But it was more than just the end of the original 'cast' of lions. It was the end of the use of trained animals in close contact work. I felt nothing but pity for those middle-aged lionesses – well, perhaps not middle-aged for captive lionesses, which can live more than twenty years. But, certainly, in the wild they would be more than halfway through their natural lifespan. We had never really developed any relationship with them – how can you at the end of a little stick? Or only touching to order? One can hardly blame them. Life in the circus trailer or cage or ring and performing on command can't be much fun. Then everything changed.

Boy and Girl, two orphan lions who had become mascots of the Scots Guards Regiment in Nairobi, came to us with their friend, Sergeant Ronald Ryves. Of the other lions, Mara and Ugas and little Elsa and her brothers, came from the Nairobi Orphanage. Henrietta came from the Orphanage in Uganda. Emperor Haile Selassie sent three little cubs from Ethiopia, and others arrived from Suki Bisletti who had some rescued lions on her property in Kenya. Our whole approach was transformed in an instant. Now it really was 'getting-to-know-you' time. And time was of the essence. Walking together, playing football, sitting around, feeding time. From early morning until bedtime we lived with them. Learned about their likes and dislikes and idiosyncrasies. How to understand what they were thinking, to see the world from their point of view. We took off our wrist guards and threw away the little sticks.

For almost two weeks Sergeant Ryves, Boy and Girl and ourselves were inseparable. Out on the plains at dawn, games of ambush on a deserted airfield some four miles from camp. Then one day the Sergeant, who had become a friend, left. Now it was just the four of us. In those early days Bill and I often used to go out with them on our own. It was heavenly. Walking with two young lions in Africa felt absolutely natural.

It was late one afternoon when we were up on the airfield that we all spotted a little group of Thomson's gazelles. Too far off to catch up with but near enough to stalk. Boy and Girl instinctively crouched, bellies touching the earth, and inched their way forward. Now and again Boy would turn back to us and tap us on the ankle, as if to say

'Come on, join in'. So we did. We got down on our hands and knees and began to crawl over the rough grass. After a while my knees began to feel sore and scratched and I stood up. At that moment, Boy turned and saw me. By now highly excited, he took a flying leap at me and knocked me down. The game was over.

As I fell I heard a loud crack and felt an excruciating pain in my ankle. Both lions stood looking down at me. Later, Bill told me he knew he had to act quickly. A few days before, Boy and Girl had been hiding in a bush and refused to come out when it was time to return to camp. Bill had taken off his shirt and ran through the grass waving it enticingly. Sure enough the lions emerged and tried to catch the fluttering cloth. Now he did the same again. He managed to lead them back to the Land Rover, tempting Boy into the back. Girl refused to go in but climbed up on the roof. Bill lifted me as gently as he could and carried me to the car. Finally, he persuaded Girl to join Boy in the back, rewarding her with some bone marrow we always took with us. I thought the journey to camp would never end.

There weren't any strong painkillers at base but I swallowed whatever I was given and wondered what would happen next. By now the light was fading, too late for a plane to come up from Nairobi and take me down. So they made me as comfortable as possible in the back of a car and we began the 125 mile journey. I remember little of that.

It was the greatest good fortune that a well-known surgeon, Garth Williams, was in Nairobi and he came as quickly as he could to operate on my ankle. It turned out to be a Pott's fracture; quite common, as I later learned, but all I could think about was getting that injection that would stop the pain. I awoke next day in a cool, white room which was to be home for a while as I had more operations and bones were re-set. I thought endlessly of Bill and the children, Boy and Girl, about being with them again, but I had to be patient. Bill drove down several times each week to see me, to bring stories of the children and the lions – and how George and he were discouraging Boy and Girl from playing rough. They knew what challenges lay ahead, as did I. But once I had learned to use the crutches I was off again. Bill took me home.

It was not only the children who were intrigued by the hard, white plaster but so, it transpired, were the lions. No-one quite knew what kind of a reception I would get. I was driven into camp just as Bill and George were bringing Boy and Girl back from a walk. I wound down the window and called. They both ran to the car, Girl jumped on the roof and Boy pushed half of his body through the window and rubbed his beautiful head against me. Oh, the warmth and comfort of that hug. He had remembered me. And so we renewed our friendship and our trust, which had never really been broken.

The plaster really was a bit of a problem, a sort of alien object that puzzled the animals. They regarded it with suspicion. In the end it was decided to make some special trousers with a zip down the inner leg, and a huge safari boot. The plaster became invisible. And it meant I could start filming, sitting down and standing still shots at least.

Apart from the need to get to work as soon as possible, Bill and I knew we shouldered an added responsibility. Although it had become obvious that this love story could never really be told with the circus lions, some people believed – possibly till the end – that this was still the best way. They were hoping to prove us wrong. I have never really understood why, but that was our challenge and we had, as a friend, the one person who made our hopes a reality. George Adamson. Without him I think we would have failed.

Every morning we rose at about 6 am, and within half an hour we met up with George down at the lions' enclosures, where we would encourage whichever animal was to be filmed that morning to jump into the back of the Land Rover. Then, out onto the awakening plains, where we walked, played football or balloons, and generally used up some of the lion's energy before returning to the set. At an agreed time we would contact the first assistant director on our walkie-talkies and arrive around 8.30 am. The crew were all gathered inside big wire cages with the camera equipment, and the morning's work would begin.

Sometimes, it was the simplest line of direction in the script that would take the longest time to film. 'Elsa sits down in the road'. It sounds easy. About an hour's work. Not at all. Elsa (Girl) did not want to lie in the sun in the road, she preferred to retreat to the shade of a tree where she was half hidden by leaves. Hours passed. The day passed. It couldn't go on!

Next morning a large trench was dug a little way off down the track. The camera was set up, George got into the trench and was covered with a few branches. Girl was enticed into position. 'Action!' George poked a shaving brush up through the branches and, miraculously, caught Girl's attention. Her eyes focused on this strange moving

Above: 'Getting to know' Astra the lioness, with trainer Monika.
Below: The moment before Boy jumps.

object, just long enough for the shot to be completed. Of course, she then went over to investigate and George was subjected to the usual effusive greeting!

It was Girl that we took down to the coast to do the swimming scenes. We soon discovered that she didn't really like the water (in spite of many days playing with balloons in a dam on our regular walks). Another problem was that I had only just had the plaster cast taken off and my foot swelled up in the heat. Luckily I wore old tennis shoes so I just cut the front of the left one open. One solution led to another.

We had also brought Mara with us so we could keep in touch with her every day (Boy too had come to join us). 'We'll try Mara in the sea,' we decided. Mara was a water baby. You couldn't get her out of the water! I still can't quite believe that Bill and I actually swam with a lioness in the ocean. If it wasn't for the film and the photos it really would be a dream.

One of the most difficult and challenging scenes was when Elsa fought with a lioness following her rehabilitation to the wild. A rocky area of land had been chosen, some distance from camp and enclosed by a high wire fence. Within this, two small areas, out of sight of each other, were prepared for the lionesses used in this scene. (Neither were animals we had close contact with). Each day one was let out into the large area for a few hours, so she established it as her territory. The filming day arrived. All necessary equipment had been set up to part the animals should it be required. Bill and I went up to watch. As he wrote in *On Playing With Lions*:

> We never realised how wild and fierce our lions could be until we saw that fight. The books we had read on the voyage out and those before, like *Maneaters of Tsavo*, had faded in our memory with our growing love and trust for our new friends, until they seemed like children's stories of fabled beasts; myths of quite another world and time.

The sight and sounds of the fight were terrifying. Our hearts were in our mouths. But neither lioness was hurt. After a lifetime of seconds one lioness retreated. The fight was over.

There was one incident that even George found extraordinary. Bill and I had taken Girl out on her own on the plains for some exercise and play. A car joined us later on bringing the director of publicity and Charles McCarry of the *Saturday Evening Post* to see what was happening.

It was a strange echo from the day Bill and I had taken the lions out before filming began, and had 'stalked' the ever-elusive Thomson gazelles: on this day too a small group of them grazed some way off. They were a little closer this time, but we thought nothing of it as the lions were orphaned as cubs and had no mother figure to teach them hunting skills. Girl was very affectionate, greeting us, moving on and then waiting for us to catch up. We suddenly saw Girl crouch, belly to the earth, and sidle through the grass towards the Tommies. In a flash she took off and in an instant had caught a young male. Bill ran over but too late, Girl's hold on the animal's throat never faltered. He didn't struggle. His final breath came quickly. Then, amazingly, Girl picked up the body and, carrying it between her front legs, carried it over to me where I was standing by the Land Rover, and laid it near my feet. She then came and greeted me.

She let us lift the soft body into the vehicle and we drove back in silence. Were we really now her pride? We can never know, but it is impossible not to believe that our friendship and bond with Girl was deep, and humbling.

We have already written in *On Playing With Lions* the story of making the film *Born Free*. The joyful, sad, difficult, frustrating, exhausting, rewarding experience that filled our life for ten and a half months. But a few painful memories remain deeper than others. And I feel I must recall them once more. Even now, 44 years later.

Apart from the lions, one of my very special and loved animals was Pati, the hyrax. I would spend a lot of time with her, feeding her with rose petals, her favourite treat. In fact there were two hyrax - one was Pati's stand-in. Pati made the most wonderful little noise in my ear as I carried her around on my shoulder. 'Tut-tut, bubble-bubble'. Or something like that! We became very attached to each other, and I was told she became quite withdrawn when I was away in hospital. The real-life Pati had died of old age. She had been a great 'nanny' to Elsa and her brothers when they first came into the Adamsons' lives. So, the scene when Pati died was a part of the film. A tragic part as it turned out. She had been given a little anaesthetic so she would be unconscious when I lifted her up in my arms. But this wasn't play-acting. She actually died as I held her. The dose had been excessive. It was unbearable. This little life ended, just for a film.

Born Free

Left: With Bill and the little hyrax Pati, who died in my arms.

Below left: Girl and her first kill.

Below right: With Boy.

Bottom: With George, Bill and Joy.

Born Free

Top: Playing volleyball with Girl at Watamu, Kenya.

Above left: With George and Mara the lioness.

Above right: Mara in Whipsnade Zoo.

Left: With Joy, meeting Kenyan President Jomo Kenyatta.

And then there was the fate of all those amazing lions and lionesses that we had got to know over the many months. Some had become friends. We had trusted them. They had trusted us. But now, we knew, most of them were going to be betrayed. Deals had been struck between the producers and safari parks and zoos in England and America. Whipsnade, Longleat, Paignton, Detroit. Thank God George and Joy had been given Boy and Girl by the Scots Guards Regiment. A letter to them from the Regimental Sergeant-Major reads: 'We have been around looking at some of the first-class zoos and we are not impressed.' Permission was given to release Boy and Girl. Eventually Ugas, although initially returned to the Nairobi Orphanage, was given to George as well, and he began his rehabilitation work in Meru with his little trio.

For our fun-loving Henrietta, there were to be no more happy lunches sharing our hard-boiled eggs and sardines. She was returned to Uganda to the zoo. She was now 'an attraction'. Mara and Little Elsa went to Whipsnade. Mara, who was our brilliant swimmer in the scenes filmed at Watamu on Kenya's East Coast. Mara with her fierce possessiveness and even fiercer affection. Little Elsa, my treasured friend, with whom I would walk alone in the bush and play hide-and-seek and just share time together. It was really a nightmare and no-one really understood our feelings except George and Joy and James Hill, our director. We were considered to be somewhat over-emotional, and that perhaps the experience had made us a bit 'extreme'. Perhaps it had.

We realised there were people out there who were not really our friends when we arrived back in London at the airport with our children and nanny, late at night. We were overjoyed to see my mother and father-in-law there to greet us, but suddenly, from behind a pillar, stepped the film's publicity director. A quick greeting, and then: 'Carl is very disappointed in you'. No amount of years can make me forget those words. Perhaps his disappointment was lessened when the film turned out to be a great success. But the rewards and priceless treasures we received from those months in Naro Muru were beyond financial gain. The animals, the Adamsons, all the kind and friendly people we got to know, or who looked after us in our house. And, perhaps the greatest gift of all, was that this experience opened up our minds and our hearts to a world we had known little about.

Virginia McKenna

When we got back Bill said that, more than anything, he wanted to make a documentary about what happened to some of the lions in *Born Free*. We pooled our savings and he made his first film, *The Lions Are Free*. The film opens with our visit to Whipsnade to see Mara and Little Elsa. I dreaded it. We saw them in the enclosure, with two other lionesses and a huge male, and I called them. They instantly looked up, ran over to me, paced the fence, reached up - moaning. We were all crying. It was six months since I had seen them. Not only elephants remember.

My memory of our *Born Free* lions haunts me to this day. Of course I remember the happy, funny and exciting times as well, but the sorrow of the banishment of most of our animal friends to life in captivity became, I believe, the foundation stone of what lay ahead for us.

The Lions Are Free was networked three times in America (although it was never shown on British television) and provided Bill with enough money to continue with his new work. Documentary film-making. Bill was an extraordinary storyteller. His use of words, his talent in all the visual aspects of film-making, made him an outstanding writer/producer and gave him the opportunity to work with some remarkable people.

Wildlife cameraman Simon Trevor, who had worked with us on *An Elephant Called Slowly*, asked Bill to produce and write two films he was making in Tsavo National Park in Kenya. One was about elephant poaching and the ivory trade, the other about the little orphans that result from this cruel and terrible practice. Bill decided that the two films should become one and he interwove the stories in a kind of counterpoint, each highlighting the other. The two main people in the story were the Sheldricks, David and Daphne. David, who fought a constant and courageous battle against the poachers, and Daphne, who tenderly and tirelessly cared for the small, living victims. She became the mother figure and, as I write, continues to be so. I cannot count the number of young elephants which owe their lives to her.

Bloody Ivory, as the film was called, received a BAFTA award nomination and Audubon Best of Festival Award in 1983. Simon and Bill went on to work together again in Simon's film *River of Sand*, describing how a four-year drought turns a river into sand and yet how life can still be sustained in that parched environment.

The Queen's Garden

WITH OXFORD SCIENTIFIC FILMS Bill made a series of documentaries. *Death Trap*, narrated on camera by the inimitable Vincent Price. *Sexual Encounters of the Floral Kind*, about pollination! And my favourite, *The Queen's Garden*.

Her Majesty graciously gave permission for a documentary on the life of the private garden at Buckingham Palace, to be filmed over the period of one year. Of course both Bill and James Hill, who continued to work with him on many productions, had been 'vetted' carefully. I remember we had a delightful, relaxed lunch with Ron Allison, at that time the Queen's Press Secretary, and we left feeling reasonably hopeful we would get the go-ahead.

It fell to me to be the Queen's 'stand-in'! She had most kindly agreed to appear in the film in a scene where she would walk through the rose garden and have a chat with Fred Nutbeam, the head gardener. We went in early and I walked the route she would take so that everything would be set up before she arrived. What fun it was, and how

Her Majesty the Queen with James Hill.

professionally and calmly Her Majesty handled it all. Leaving us, she remarked – I sensed with a slight reluctance – that she then had to go and sit for another portrait painting. It can't always be much fun, I thought. To our joy, the Queen liked the film. Bill and James were invited to a private showing with her at the Palace and, I learned afterwards, it was one of the films she had on board *Britannia* when she travelled the seas.

This privileged glimpse into the royal garden's life was richly enhanced by the stunning background music composed by John Scott. It is an integral part of the film and, for me, one of the most brilliant documentary film scores I have ever heard.

Bill did a further series with Jane Goodall and Hugo van Lawick, her first husband, who was a leading wildlife cameraman. *The Baboons of Gombe*: the story of a wild troop that lived near Jane's chimpanzee research camp in Tanzania (then Tanganyika); *The Hyena Story*, the film that changed my ill-informed view of hyenas as mean scavengers to one of understanding and appreciation of their caring and strong parental characteristics; *Lions of the Serengeti*, life in the wild for lions with all its fierce and family dimensions. Finally, *The Wild Dogs of Africa*, famous for the survival story of little Solo on the Serengeti Plains. All these films went out under the heading of *Jane Goodall and the World of Animal Behaviour*.

With Krov and Ann Menuhin, Bill made *A Prospect of Whales*, remembered for a dramatic moment when Anne, swimming near a 60-foot whale, is caught and swept into the air by its giant tail fluke.

I was so lucky to have met and got to know all these adventurous, creative and extraordinary people, at the forefront in the world of wildlife documentary film-making. In the 1970s and '80s wildlife issues had not captured the interest and imagination as they were to do subsequently. It means a lot to me that Bill was so successful in this field, and it became a great asset in our later work. Through meeting so many animal and conservation experts, he became informed in a very deep and personal way.

And then, finally and especially, there was *Christian: The Lion at World's End* (whose story appears on pages 113-19). Initially Bill had made two films – *The Lion at World's End* and *Christian: the Lion* – which were eventually edited together. This is the film from which an extract was recently shown on YouTube and received around 30 million 'hits'. The moment when Christian recognised and greeted Ace and John after not having seen them for almost a year. This fragment of film, shot nearly 40 years ago, has kindled a feeling, a sympathy, between the animal world and the viewing public, now more accustomed to 'game shows', reality TV and soaps, that is truly thrilling. How George would have chuckled. How Bill would have smiled. Deep inside us we need this connection, this realisation that we are all animals, that we all in our different ways have feelings, and experience joy, grief, anger, jealousy. Many of us who work in the world of animal welfare, wildlife protection and conservation, feel we are in a frightening minority. Perhaps Christian can restore a balance, perhaps his spirit, together with Elsa's, can create a more sensitive and compassionate approach towards the creatures who, tragically, are always at our mercy.

I can't think why I wrote 'at our mercy'. Mercy is the last thing we show them. Is it merciful to trap them, shoot them for 'fun', train them to do tricks, confine them in cages, trailers, keep them as 'pets' in apartments, trade them or their body parts, condemn them to a lifetime of captivity? The quality of our mercy is indeed very strained. How I love Walt Whitman's poem 'I think I could turn and live with animals…' and how happy I am that, for a brief while, I did.

In a strange way I think that actors can be peculiarly sensitive to animals. The senses of actors are heightened, acute, and perhaps their awareness of the emotions, thoughts and feelings of their colleagues in performance would be very similar to that of the non-human animals' awareness of each other. Body language, eye contact, alertness to unexpected reactions. Words play no part in those.

To the Rescue!

UTUMN WILL SOON BE here. Perhaps it has already started: grey skies, high winds beating branches with unripened acorns to the ground, coolness. I am in a strangely symbiotic state with the weather. A slow change of gear in which I approach the final stages of these scribblings and the last hours, days, years – who knows – of my life. Of course I might live to a great age, but 'sans teeth...sans everything'? Doesn't sound too exciting, although it is touching to be remembered while you are still alive! The old films or stage shows that some people enjoyed occasionally prompt them to come up to me as I'm shopping or waiting for a train. And to be recognised after all those years is pretty wonderful! It is usually the animal films that they want to talk about, but from time to time *The King and I*, *The Smallest Show on Earth*, *A Town Like Alice*, *Carve Her Name with Pride* and even Rosalind in *As You Like It* at the Old Vic get us chatting away.

I was still acting when we started Zoo Check in 1984, working with Roger Rees, Kenneth Branagh, Brian Blessed and Frances Barber in *Hamlet* at Stratford-on-Avon. What a cast! I was just in the one play, so stayed up at Stratford for rehearsals and then commuted every so often once the play opened. I loved every minute of it, felt very privileged, and the pleasure of staying in Shakespeare's birthplace made each day a gift.

Bill came up for the opening and whenever he could, and we had jolly evenings in The Dirty Duck, opposite the theatre, favourite haunt of the actors after the show. We transferred to the Barbican, in London, the following year, but it wasn't quite the same.

In 1984 Bill, assisted by our sons Will and Justin, was fully into his documentary film-making. For some years we had a wonderful studio in Flood Street, off the King's Road in Chelsea, but his work demands outgrew the space. Sadly, as we both loved it there so much.

He then bought one of the old Turner studios in Glebe Place. It was stunning, with a huge living area and several small rooms on a gallery which served as offices. But it didn't have the peace of the first studio and I never really enjoyed staying there for the night.

So it was, in that same year, that we had to find another office for Zoo Check. A tiny one, as we had very little money. Tempo House in Battersea was perfect. One very small room, furnished with a table, two chairs, a filing cabinet, a telephone, a writing pad and some pens. Peopled by volunteers, of which I was one. Will often used to fly across the bridge in his lunch break to see what was happening and if he could help. It was a very exciting, if challenging, time – for me still very busy in *Hamlet* at Stratford, taking armfuls of letters and stationery with me when I travelled up for performances.

We stayed at Tempo House until April 1985. Work was growing. By a stroke of good luck a cottage we had across our garden was empty, and Bill had the brilliant idea of bringing the office there. Instead of an hour's drive I could walk to work in two minutes. Surrounded by nature, it was the perfect setting for our animal charity.

We are very fortunate as a considerable number of the people who work with us have been around a long time. Tricia Holford for twenty-five years. At the start she lived in and ran the office. Then, as the years passed, every room became an office and we had to create more space by putting up large chalets in the garden. Finally, ten years ago we were bursting at the seams and moved to an office in Horsham. Still the pulse of Born Free. The loyal and dedicated people in our team bring so much energy and commitment to the Foundation's work. Anne Tudor, Shirley Galligan, Alison Hood, Mandy Ford and Celia Nicholls, who have been with us for years, and a younger stream, bright, enthusiastic and committed. Our talented Trustee Board. And motivating us all, articulate, knowledgeable, tireless and always approachable is our CEO, Will. All of them, including our volunteers, encourage and inspire us in their different ways, keeping the spirit of Elsa alive.

People sometimes ask me if I could ever have imagined that our work would grow to the extent it has. Of course, the answer is no. Does one ever think of the future in that way? We just thought what we thought and did what we did and, gradually, more and more people believed in us, helped us, identified with us. Our responsibilities grew simultaneously, to the animals, of course, but also to the supporters who trusted us to translate thought into action.

A thought which does not result in an action is nothing much, and an action which does not proceed from a thought is nothing at all.

Prince Sadruddin Aga Khan (1983)

How succinctly put!

Roger Rees and I then began our *Sons and Mothers* programmes. I began taking small groups on safari – the first to Zambia, followed by one with Bill to India, and then off and on to East Africa and once more to India until 2006. In between there were small parts in films, television films, poetry readings, my final theatre production *Winnie* and some writing. Life was full. Zoo Check was growing, as was the number of our projects. We were now taking on animals-in-the-wild issues as well as the captivity agenda: Zoo Check became The Born Free Foundation.

My thought that actors and actresses (yes, I still like to call us that!), and others in the entertainment and sporting worlds, are sensitive to animals has been borne out by the fact that several of them have joined us and supported us over the years. And not just as a name on a piece of paper. Martin Clunes, Joanna Lumley, Jenny Seagrove, Helen Worth, Amanda Holden, Martin Shaw, Nigel Havers, Angela Rippon, John Altman, Anneka Rice, Rula Lenska, Tony Britton, Sandi Toksvig, Brian Blessed, Liz Fraser, Andrew Lynford. So many have found time in their busy lives to come to events, help us in whatever way they can. A very particular kind of generosity. I remember, too, people who are no longer with us. The late Robin Cook and Tony Banks, always finding time in their pressured government lives to unstintingly advise and support us. That meant so much .

I shall always remember our very first fund-raising evening in 1984. It was at the Queen's Elm pub on the Fulham Road. An old friend of Bill's, Sean Treacy, who organised the drinks for us at our wedding in 1957, offered us the room upstairs at the pub as a venue for an art auction. Elizabeth Frink gave us a beautiful drawing of a horse. The generosity of people we hardly knew was incredible. And for our auctioneer we had one of showbiz's most loved perform-ers. Ronnie Corbett. He was tremendous, and twenty-four years on Ronnie is still helping us. Mark Ramprakash has chosen Born Free as one of his Testimonial Year charities to support and is holding a *Strictly Come Dancing* event at the Hilton. Ronnie is part of it, and

Above: With Ronnie Corbett and Joanna Lumley at Zoo Check's first fund-raising evening in 1984.

Left: Rachel Hunter with a family of gorillas in Uganda.

Bottom left: Helen Worth feeding Pinkie, an orphaned baby elephant, in Sri Lanka.

Below: Martin Clunes and Amanda Holden in a Britannia Airways in-flight film for the Born Free Foundation.

drawing the raffle. The loyalty, the belief in what we do is overwhelming. In their busy lives Ronnie, Mark, Graham Norton, Rachel Hunter, Bryan Adams, Fiona Phillips, Billie Piper – and many more – have found the time and care enough to help in our work. Some are very hands-on, like Jenny and Joanna, Amanda and Helen, Martin, Rachel and Anneka – all of whom have helped with rescues. Then there are others. Often unsung.

Supporters of Born Free who continuously and amazingly spread the word, put on fund-raising events. No effort is spared. It seems they can never do enough, and it all comes from the heart. Two such people are Val Hackett and Mike Carey, who have put on a Ball in Derby for nine consecutive years. A massive undertaking as we all know. Their auctioneer, each year, is James Lewis – of TV's *Flog It* and *Cash in the Attic* fame, who doesn't spare himself to raise the roof with his auctioneering technique; I wish my father could have seen him! And Angela and Martin Humphery, who support several charities and each year organise a fund-raising lunch at their home. There are too many to mention but in schools, in homes, in big and small ways, young people, old people and those in between demonstrate to us how much they care. I find it inspiring.

IT IS the rescues that bring the heart of our work into focus and touch the human heart. The plight of the individual animal. And through that individual, we can draw attention to the plight of hundreds of others that we are unable to help.

Rescues involve risk. Of course, the animals are always given a thorough health check by our vet, John Knight, before they are pronounced fit to travel. But that isn't the whole story. Animals that have been kept in poor conditions for a long time are vulnerable. Their health monitoring, their diet, their living conditions have been desperately inadequate, quite apart from any social aspect of their lives: animals that should live in pairs or family groups, existing in solitude. Several have come to us with liver and kidney problems, calcium deficiency, others with intense fear and dislike of humans; others, with perhaps only a short time to live, we have still decided to help, so that at least the final months or few years of life would be comfortable. A way of saying sorry for all the rest.

There was one lioness that we all remember. 1997, Kimba. She survived only one month after living all her life in a cage on an Italian hillside. Bought as a cub by her owner as a gift to his son, she soon became too strong and into the cage she went. There was no separate side area, so it was never cleaned out. Her food was chicken or meat still on their polystyrene trays from the supermarket. She lived on a mountain of faeces and rubbish. I need not describe what it was like.

We knew the risk was high, but we couldn't bear to leave her there, her head bowed, her back sunken, her hind legs wasted. So we brought her to a Sanctuary in Kent. She walked on grass for the first time in fourteen years, felt the clear air, slept on straw, ate good food. She was loved. For three weeks all seemed to be well. Then she became critically lethargic. An enlarged spleen. It was removed, to give her a chance. Medically speaking, she died from cancer of the immune system, centred in her spleen, but she really died from years of malnutrition and neglect. How tragically brief was our chance to say sorry.

The first rescue we ever did, in 1995, was of two lions and a leopard. In Tenerife. Island of holidays and fun and sunshine. Stuck in cages on the roof of a bar were these three animals. British people are fantastic when it comes to animals. Yes, of course, there is a downside: badger-baiting and hunting and trapping and puppy farms and dogs on chains, vivisection and factory farming. All of that and more. But when people see an animal is suffering in some way then phone calls, letters, faxes – and now emails – come hurtling into our office.

I had received letters about these animals from visitors to Tenerife during the whole of the five years it took us to rescue them. We called the lions Raffi and Anthea (after Anthea Turner who was, at that time, a presenter on *GMTV* and very supportive of what we were doing). The leopard was Rikki.

My son, Daniel, had gone to Tenerife on a job and went to see the roof cages for us. He couldn't believe what he saw. There was no permanent water supply for the animals to drink from – and a roof top in Tenerife is not the coolest of places – so they had to wait until the owner climbed up on the cages and poured water from a can into their desperate mouths. Movement was restricted. Two or three paces; turn; or lie on a narrow wooden plank with nails protruding from it. Nails that had wounded Anthea. We knew from our experience of taking the six ex-circus tigers to our Sanctuary in India, and of returning the last three captive dolphins from England to even-

Right: Anthea and Raffi in their roof cage in Tenerife.

Below: Anthea and Raffi in the Julie Ward Centre, Shamwari.

Bottom left: Kimba in her cage on the Italian hillside.

Bottom right: Kimba in a BFF-funded sanctuary in Kent.

tual freedom in the Caribbean, that rescues are fraught with frustrations and problems. And are extremely expensive. But once we make a decision, nothing will stop us.

The government in Tenerife showed little inclination to respond to our repeated communications until, following a fantastic article in *The Mail on Sunday* and a feature on *GMTV*, they suddenly leapt into action. The story is a long one, but finally the lions and the leopard (who had been de-clawed) came to the Kent Sanctuary. Britannia Airways, which was also to help with Kimba, flew them all to England. Two years later they were at Shamwari, in South Africa, the first of our lions to experience their rightful environment in the bush. Not a free one but a natural one.

I wrote in our *Wildlife Times* of Spring/Summer 1997:

> I was unashamedly emotional when Anthea and Raffi stepped, at last, onto the African soil and I knew they had finally 'come home'. Without question this has been, for me, the happiest outcome of all our endeavours over the years. We could never have dreamed that one day, the lions' tiny cement and barred cell would be transformed into three acres of African bush. But, sometimes, with the help of friends, dreams do come true.

And Rikki was to join them and lived, happily, for a further four years.

When Raffi and Anthea died in 2006 they were buried, as others had been, in the garden at the Julie Ward Centre at Shamwari. Each grave is marked with a tree instead of a stone. Our memories of all the amazing, courageous animals to whom we have had the good fortune to give a second chance in life will never be buried. They are living and giving us strength to continue.

As I think about the animals I never forget the people. I have sometimes heard it said that people who are mad about animals don't give a damn about people. I find that a bit crazy, I have to say! Bill summed it up for me - and I think for many others - when he wrote:

> It is not that I am more interested in animals than humans. I am just interested in life.

Conversely, I have come across people who never give a moment's thought to animals. And then there are people who take a kind of middle road - 'Oh, I love animals', but don't mind seeing them in zoos and circuses, or birds in cages, or dolphins in concrete pools performing tricks, or seeing TV programmes about lots of baby animals being born in zoos (I wonder where they all end up), or places called 'Sanctuaries' which, in reality, are commercial businesses, where breeding and selling is par for the course.

I have mentioned Shamwari a couple of times and our Rescue and Rehabilitation Centres in South Africa. Thanks to the enormous generosity of Jean Byrd, a South African lady living in Durban who had visited our Julie Ward Centre, we now have a second one, in the north of the Park.

How did this all come about? It began about fourteen years ago when we were introduced to the owner of Shamwari, Adrian Gardiner, by a senior staff member of wonderful Britannia Airways. I think Adrian was intrigued by our rescue work and, following meetings and discussions, he said we could build a centre in Shamwari.

In 1988 Julie Ward, a lovely young English girl, was murdered in the Maasai Mara Game Reserve in Kenya. To this day her father, John, relentlessly strives to bring the guilty party to justice. Ten years afterwards Julie's mother, Jan, encouraged by her friends, and friends of Julie's from her youth - notably the musician Carmelo Luggeri - expressed a deep wish to do something to commemorate her life and all she stood for. Wild places and wild animals were her passion and so, with us at Born Free, *The Mail on Sunday* and Olympus cameras, an exhibition of Julie's photographs and excerpts from her letters home was mounted in London, accompanied by a book, *Gentle Nature*, which Nick Buckley had edited from Julie's words and pictures. The opening was a very stirring event and even those of us who had not known Julie were moved and entranced by her images of Africa and its creatures. As her daughter had been inspired by that incredible land, Jan had been touched by the story of our rescue of the two lions, Anthea and Raffi, from Tenerife. They were now living at Shamwari and we were planning the move there of Rikki, the Tenerife roof-top leopard - now at the Kent Sanctuary - and the rescue of two lions from a cage in the National Gardens in Athens. Aslan and Gilda.

We wanted Julie's name to be kept alive, for her love of animals to inspire others, and so it was that in September 1999 the Julie Ward Education and Rescue Centre was opened. Jan planted a tree, Kiki Dee accompanied by Carmelo sang the song 'Born Free' and several of Julie's friends, Adrian Gardiner and the Shamwari team, Helen Worth and many of us from Born Free gathered round. A priest blessed the animals and the Centre.

The cruel fire that had been lit to try (unsuccessfully) to destroy Julie's remains has been replaced by a bright, warming trail of sparks that opens our awareness of the suffering of innocent animals and stirs our compassion, our understanding and our wish to care for them.

Adrian Gardiner is a very interesting person. Having bought a huge property with land not far from Port Elizabeth as a holiday retreat, he then became fired with a passion to fill the land with wildlife. He bought up tired old farmland that surrounded him, allowed it to revert to bush, and eventually reintroduced wild animals that had been indigenous to that area in days gone by. Shamwari now covers over 25,000 hectares (61,776 acres). It has wild herbivores of all kinds. And predators too, cheetah, leopards and lions, and beautiful elephants; and wide-eyed children. Creating awareness in the children about their environment, their wildlife (most of which these young people have never previously seen), is a huge and important aspect of our presence and work at the Centres. The school classes are bussed in, our team tells them about the behaviour and way of life of the animals and their natural environment. They are then taken to see our rescued big cats and their life stories explained. Finally, they visit the Reserve to experience nature as a whole. The bugs and birds, giraffes and warthogs, rhinos, hippos and all the rest. I feel such joy that we have been able to open a new window for these children, a chance to experience a different aspect of life to tell their parents about. Who knows but they may grow up to be teachers or rangers and the message of understanding and compassion will be passed on. Must be passed on. Without it, the animals are doomed and, so, spiritually, are we.

Leopard

That look of scorn and anger burned my soul.
The yellow orbs shone cold gold metal.
My throat closed up. I turned my head away.

Black panthers in the forest move with silken stealth
Between the trees
Feet silent as they touch the fallen leaves.
Bodies are tuned like springs
For hunting, seeking a mate, guarding their territory.
Life is dangerous, but meant to be that way.

Here at Lai Chi Kok there is no forest, no fallen leaves
No night of stars, no rains, no warming sun.
The cage of concrete, ceilinged with the same.
Allows no patterns of the light to change
The monotone of grey in that cold cell.

The shining coat of wilder days has gone
Now dry, worn thin and lifeless like the body it encases.
The crowd screams round and shouts and roars its joy.
I also scream inside my head and shout.
This wasted tragic death in life
Is one more horror to haunt me in the night.
And fifty feet away the funfair and the music
Blast raucously to split your ears.
And no-one gives a damn.

This zoo in Hong Kong has been closed many years. The leopard, long dead, has gone to a kinder place. But, tragically, the ignorance, the lack of understanding about what captivity means to a wild creature, are alive and well. Only yesterday I heard a discussion on the radio about conservation breeding of tigers in zoos. It was described as responsible breeding – different, it was stated, from the breeding 'farms' in the Far East, where tigers are mass-bred for skins and body parts. It is true that the reasons are different but, for the tigers, the differences are difficult to distinguish. They are still captive, without choice, dependent on humans. Perhaps living in a larger enclosure, but still captive.

It was admitted that reintroduction to the wild was an imponderable. After all, in twenty, thirty, forty years' time, will there really be *more* wild habitat for them? What was really being acknowledged was that conservation breeding is what philosopher Mary Midgley in her chapter in our book *Beyond the Bars* (1987) describes as 'Keeping Species on Ice'. We know that, as far as tigers are concerned, breeding is not a problem. But there are many associated complications – sustaining a varied gene pool, ensuring all the zoos which are part of the 'programme' have 'acceptable' facilities for the animals. Everything, in a way, is artificial.

Perhaps we should applaud the candour of biologist and writer Jeremy Cherfas, who wrote in 1984:

> Quite honestly there can be no rational reason for saving wildlife in zoos. The best reason to conserve animals in zoos is simply that it gives us pleasure.

If only we could persuade people that conservation in the wild and of the wild is the only reasonable solution to maintaining a balanced world, or the downward path is inevitable. Science is clever, but nature knows best.

I SUPPOSE the debate, to have or not to have zoos, boils down to my personal priority. Do I care more about criticism? My view being perceived as extreme? 'How could you not want little Johnny to see a live elephant, a lion, a monkey – to see nearly all animal life in one place?' Or do I care more about conserving the balance of nature and about the individual animal? Its well-being is what matters to me, physically, socially and psychologically. I am, of course, acutely aware of how 'dressing up' can be deceptive. As an actress, the coat on your back, the hat on your head, your stylish shoes, your bright lipstick, can create an impression deeply at odds with the reality of the person inside the clothes. That is illusion.

In a way, the 'dressing up' done by many zoos in recent times is no different. The audience is beguiled by some grass, a tree or two, a climbing frame, a moat instead of bars. By talk of breeding for conservation. It can be most convincing, and, yes, it is 'better' than a concrete cage.

But look beyond. Look inside. Look through. Strip away the scenery, the greenery; the reality, the problem for the animal is the same. Captivity.

THERE ISN'T a single day that passes that I don't think about the animals in Pata Store Zoo. I had hoped we could have had an action plan in place for later this year, but I was too optimistic. A day in the life of those animals, mirrored in so many other zoos around the world, doesn't bear contemplating. We have moved forward, inch by inch, and I know we will jump into action eventually. With the Thai government in a state of flux nothing is certain. It is an unwelcome waiting game.

It is probably hard for people who aren't particularly interested in or involved with animals, to understand how deep our commitment goes. When Bill turned seventy he could have opted for an armchair role, picked up his pen and just written about his thoughts and views. But he didn't. He couldn't.

In the early 1990s, with Gervase Farjeon, he filmed and compiled the most indisputable and comprehensive examples of disturbed behaviour in captive wild animals. The editor, Joe Phillips, turned the footage they had amassed over several years into the *Zoochotic Report*, on which our 1994 *Zoo Inquiry* was based. It caused quite a stir. I don't suppose such an explicit and focused film had been made on the subject before.

He couldn't rest unless he was out there, filming, recording, bringing back the pictures. The evidence. 'Inadmissible Evidence' is the title

of his chapter in *Beyond the Bars*. Just look at the headlines announcing the death of this lovely elephant, Pole Pole, at London Zoo.

Twenty-four years on, what has been learned, what has changed? It is only when I feel that the answer is 'very little' that I occasionally feel desperately inadequate. We never seem to make much progress up the cliff-face we have chosen to climb, and I feel an acute sense of sadness.

I think it is quite easy to disappear
If you are still and hardly breathe
Hardly anyone will notice you.

In other times I thought I would mind
Being invisible
Now I'm not so sure.

And of course nothing stays the same
The seasons don't so why should we.

The soft green lace of spring soon turns
To dazzling summer and autumn's glowing reds
Quite soon reveal the vulnerable shapes
Of winter boughs.

When you are young the sword of your ideals
Is always bright
Always at the ready.
You really did believe the world needed you
And it made you feel like an angel
On horseback.

Now I think I can serve it best
By taking up as little space
As a body needs.

In any case
They're cutting all the trees
Soon we won't know what the season is.

But these moments are transitory and few. My ideals still light the way. My hopes for a kinder world.

I refuse to be a pessimist. I refuse to believe that the wild must vanish. That zoos are the only answer. I refuse to accept that in my lifetime, and my children's lifetime, the last wild black rhino will be poached for its horn, the last tract of rainforest was levelled for cattle ranching and the last whale was turned into a bar of soap. And that I stood by and did nothing about it.

Planet Earth

WHAT IS THIS FEELING we call 'spiritual'? Is it that undefinable deep awareness, unrelated to any particular belief or religion, that is hard to describe or to explain? Sometimes it can draw us into an instinctive sympathy with others. Sometimes it seems to be a profound consciousness of a world beyond the one we know. Yet, it isn't separate from the natural world. It is when I am 'in' nature that I sense it so strongly. It puts everything in perspective, restores a balance without which we and all creatures have no future.

At this particular moment the world is terrifyingly out of balance, its sweet bells are truly 'jangled, out of tune and harsh'. Alexander Pope summed it up so aptly in his *Essay on Man*, Epistle II:

Chaos of thought and passion, all confus'd.
Still by himself abused, or disabus'd.
Created half to rise, and half to fall;
Great Lord of all things, yet a prey to all;
Sole judge of truth, in endless error hurl'd:
The glory, jest and riddle of the world!

Some are bubble blowers
Some are bubble breakers

Have you blown bubbles
In the countryside?

The world's a bubble too

One day someone will come along
And prick the world.

Virginia McKenna

The world is groaning with its pain, its wounds. Can't we hear it? With our greed and our political machinations we are squandering this treasure trove we call the planet. A sticking plaster here, a bandage there; fine words of reassurance – Trust me, 'follow me' scattered like Smarties to sweeten the disillusionment, the failures. With all the talk of tolerance, there has never been such prejudice. The childhood innocence and freedom of *Swallows and Amazons* are gone forever. Health and safety, with its crazy chains of rules undermining the simplest of pleasures, banishes joy from our hearts at the stroke of a pen. Life is filled with bruises and scratches and we have to learn how to deal with them. Face them.

Saving the Children

THERE CAN BE FEW communities further removed from ours than the one I visited in Colombia. Children facing death threats, not conkers falling off trees.

Through a journalist neighbour of mine I had had the good fortune to meet a remarkable man who had come to give a talk at the prep school our sons had attended years before. I was to introduce him. Jaime Jaramillo, a wealthy geophysicist and oil exploration consultant in Bogotá, had had an experience in 1973 that turned his world upside down. That changed his life.

Walking in the city one day, he saw a cardboard box being thrown out of a car window as it drove along. A little ragged girl dashed out into the road to pick it up. She turned, smiled at him and was then knocked down and killed by another car. The cardboard box was empty.

The little girl was one of hundreds of street children in Bogotá, some living in the sewers; some becoming teenage mothers; in appalling circumstances. Jaime found out about these hidden ghettos and determined to help them, somehow.

Over the years he had founded several homes. Sanctuaries for these young, wild humans, hundreds of whom had been victims of 'cleaning up' raids by the police. Shot as vermin. Driven to drugs, to stealing. Driven to desperation. Here, in safety, with good food, a healthy, clean environment, education, skills training, the children learn to understand that there are kind, caring and loving people in the world. There are people they can trust. They can learn to smile again.

Now a Patron of the Children of the Andes foundation, I went with the journalist Donna Leigh to Bogotá in 1991 and travelled, with Papa Jaime, to the Children of the Andes home in Cajica outside the city. The cries of joy when the children saw 'Papa' were hugely touching – as was their sweet greeting of Donna and myself. The sleeping area, the kitchen and dining room, the classrooms: all were proudly shown to us and I felt so privileged to be even a tiny fragment of such humanitarian and vital work.

Virginia McKenna

The plan had been to take us down the sewers, appropriately kitted out in rubber boots and mackintoshes but, to my disappointment, we did not go. The rains had been excessive and at such times there is always a chance that the water in the sewer pipes will flood. It was considered too high a risk. But what we did do was drive around the city at night so Jaime could check for any children sleeping in door-ways, to whom he could give food and, above all, some words of kind-ness. We found huddled shapes here and there and Jaime jumped out to do what he could to help. Along one narrow street we came across a small crowd standing on one pavement watching, on the other side, a man and a woman having a fierce and terrible argument. He was waving a gun around in the air. Jaime stopped the car and walked towards them talking in a loud, calm voice. Gradually the fighting stopped, the tension eased. It could, so easily, have ended differently.

Jaime will always be one of my heroes. He could have walked away in those early days and done nothing. He had a lovely wife, two chil-dren, a comfortable life. But that little tragic victim with her empty box opened the door to the rest of his life. Rather as Pole Pole did for us.

Children of the Andes has grown and developed over the years. Jaime still, for me, the founding inspiration.

EVEN LONGER ago, in the early 1980s, I was invited by the fostering charity Plan to become the first 'foster parent' in Kenya. I was thrilled at this chance to do something for a Kenyan family. And so little Elijah, aged six, came into my life. As I went to Kenya fairly often I had the ideal opportunity to visit 'my' family, which I did three times. Once with Bill, once with Will and once on my own. Plan was doing vital work in Gachoka District, near Embu. Schools; an Aids orphan-age; women's projects. A housing community where the bricks and the houses were actually made by the women. Health clinics. Boreholes. Help with food in times of drought.

One of my visits coincided with a severe shortage of food, and Plan had organised lunchtime meals at the school. I helped ladle nourish-ing soup from huge pans into the children's little bowls. A lifeline which lit up their vulnerable faces.

Above: My Plan-sponsored child Elijah.

Right: With Elijah and his family in Kenya.

Below: Martin Clunes gives out school uniforms in Ol Moti School in Amboseli as part of the BFF Global Friends project.

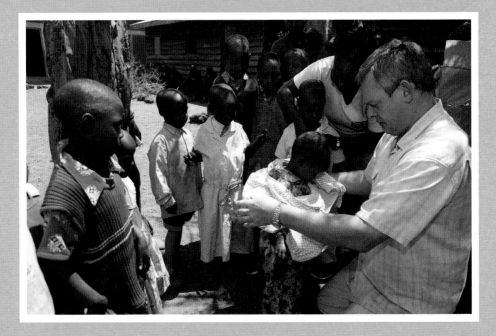

Elijah's family walked four kilometres to fetch water in those hard times. Such times meant they also had to eat their seed grain when the crops failed. I remember, on my first visit, they showed me their two little dwellings. One was their home, in which they slept, cooked, ate, lived their life. The other was their grain store. In that year they were, in fact, eating their seed grain. The future was grim.

I took simple gifts when I visited them: cotton fabric and needles and thread for Elijah's mother to make clothes. A shawl for the grandmother. Tea, sugar, flour, rice, oil, fresh fruit and vegetables, a skipping rope, a ball, some toys – things that were useful and things that were fun. I shall never forget the moment they were saying goodbye after the second visit. James, the father, came to me with a little wisp of paper inside which nestled three eggs. A meal for that family. I was deeply touched but managed to explain that it was really difficult for me to take them on the journey as they might break. He wasn't offended.

Then, when Elijah became eighteen, my sponsorship ended. I couldn't bear the thought of leaving the family so I decided to sponsor Faith, his little sister. This continued until 2003 when Plan withdrew from their work in the area, a sure sign of success as they had managed to establish a self-supporting community. But sad for me on a personal level. I felt very happy the little family now had a better house and a little more land, but I knew I would miss them. Indeed, I have never forgotten them.

However, I stayed with Plan and now sponsor fourteen-year-old Nyamani Chipwa, who lives in a very poor community on the Kenyan east coast. There is still a lot of work to do there on every level but, again, it is a privilege to have a personal involvement, even in a small way. He sends me little drawings and messages through a translator and tells me he is doing well at school. I pray this will help him to have some opportunities in the future. But water, sanitation, hygiene are still huge problems. Basic survival issues that so many millions of people have to face, which we take for granted.

IT SEEMS to me that we are always erecting barriers. Whether cultural, religious, emotional, familial, prejudicial. I have never been able to understand why. Although perhaps I have sometimes been too harsh in my criticism of others and this, occasionally, has led to an invisible barrier rising between us, I have tried, during my life, to be more tolerant and understanding. I think I can now say at my advanced age that I bear no ill will. That I accept people as they are, as I hope they accept me. There is, however, one exception. If I become aware of an incident of wilful cruelty to any creature, human or animal, I will be their defender in whatever way I can.

In the work we do at Born Free there could be a perceived barrier because people think we help animals, not people. When we started this was true. But now we embrace all life. And that is as it should be. In different ways we are all victims or beneficiaries of circumstance, of political decisions, of the whims of our law-makers, of natural disasters, of the elements. Our project Global Friends puts an arm around wild animals and the places they live in and around those people who live near them, who share that patch of the world.

We have these Global Friends projects in several African countries and two years ago I went to the community bordering on Amboseli National Park, in Kenya, with our Patron, Martin Clunes. He had already named a baby elephant born in Amboseli some years before after his own daughter, Emily Kate. So Martin was there to seek Emily Kate (and he found her!) and come to Ol Moti school with us. There was no water, broken windows in the school building, no boarding facility so the children had to walk up to seven kilometres to and from school each day. (Can you imagine that happening here?).

Two years ago Ol Moti had seventy-four pupils, two teachers, some rundown classrooms and desks. Now there are 233 children with 130 boarders – boys and girls. Seven teachers and a dining hall. They learn their lessons and they learn that there is great benefit from respecting and protecting the wild environment and its inhabitants. So when Martin came to meet the children he not only brought little school dresses for the girls, but he brought hope. He personally gave £6,000 for the rebuilding of the school. Such a gift means more than gold.

And now there is water too.

'At Peace', She Said

I WAS NOT WITH BILL when he died. The pain of that is still with me. Why do I write this? Why do I tell this? Who knows. Perhaps because there are thousands of women like me who were not there, arrived too late, had just gone out. One reads about the family round the bed, the last moments shared, the comfort received by the one slipping away. And you know the person who was the other half of yourself had none of that. You never forget it, however much you eventually get up and get on with life.

We had been to Liverpool to go on the *Richard and Judy* show, to talk about zoos. When it finished we sat down for a few moments. 'Did my voice sound odd?' Bill asked. 'No, it was fine, why?' He told me he had the most severe chest pain. We spent the two or three hours before catching our return flight sitting, slowly walking round a picture gallery. He bought Will a tie. The flight seemed eternal. I knew he was in pain and was relieved when he said he would call in at Gatwick Park Hospital on the way home. I ran to get the car. But he changed his mind. He wanted to go home.

The complication to this story was that that evening we were going to London to take an old American friend of ours, Joey Thompson, and her granddaughter to the theatre. Joey was in a wheelchair and we knew she had been looking forward to it for a long time. 'Phone Justin and ask him to go with you.' So I did. I made Bill some tea, changed, and left him at our dining table, sitting quietly. It was agony having to go out.

As a precaution I had phoned Will, who was on his way back from London, and asked him to call in to see Dad as he hadn't felt well. Just as a precaution. Bill died before he arrived.

He had gone to bed. He had gone to sleep forever. Our wonderful kind doctor, Lizzie Sells, told me later he looked peaceful. Not in distress.

Will was then faced with a terrible dilemma. Should he get a message to the theatre? That was ruled out. So, leaving Joey and her granddaughter at their hotel and saying goodnight to Justin, I drove home.

As I turned down into our steep little lane I had a strange premonition. The gate was open. A police car was there. Will and Daniel walked up to meet me. Justin rushed down from London. I stayed with Bill, all night.

Louise and her family came from Australia for the funeral in our little church. I think I was on autopilot. There was a lot to do. To arrange. As everyone knows. And, of course, as everyone knows, nothing is ever quite the same. If he was still alive he would be eighty-six. Next Friday it is our fifty-first wedding anniversary and I am going to dinner with Justin and Charlotte. He was a deep, complex man, sometimes uncompromising. But each year I celebrate his life because he gave so much, to me and the family, to his beloved Gurkhas in the war, to the animals. Some people remember him as 'a gentle giant'. To me he was a giant among men.

Anniversary

I have no gifts nor precious toy
To mark this special day.
No flowers, no fruits, no sweetmeats rare
No songs for you to play.

The only thing I have to give
Is of a doubtful hue –
Some black, some grey, a little white
Some red, some dark deep blue.

Upon my outstretched hand it lies
This present from your wife
Please take it and its pain, its joy
It's – with my love – my life.

The Far East

I AM ON A TRAIN home from Waterloo. The English countryside flashes by. This is the countryside that Gurkha soldiers would like to call home after years of service in the British Army; at least some of them would, but if they had retired prior to 1997 they are not allowed to remain in the UK. Even more extraordinary, a 91-year-old veteran Gurkha who had wished to come to this land for vital medical treatment was obliged to obtain a visa, which was to cost him £500, impossible on a small Gurkha pension in Nepal. Some veterans have no pension at all! There are thirteen VCs amongst these brave men.

I had just joined a demonstration outside the High Court in the Strand. This impressive gathering, organised by Peter Carroll – a Lib Dem MP – was spearheaded by Joanna Lumley, whose father had served in the Gurkhas. The crowd adored her. There was a tangible sense of outrage, shared by us all, that these fine, loyal men were being treated so shabbily. What price self-sacrifice? What price loyalty? The 91-year-old veteran was there, in his wheelchair. I wanted so much to shake his hand, and I will always remember this day, and the privilege I felt supporting the cause of such decent, honourable people.

Professor Sir Ralph Turner, in the Preface to his *Dictionary of the Nepali Language*, writes:

> As I write these last words, my thoughts return to you who were my comrades, the stubborn and indomitable peasants of Nepal. Once more I hear the laughter with which you greeted every hardship. Once more I see you in your bivouacs or about your fires, now shivering with wet and cold, now scorched by a piti-less and burning sun. Uncomplaining you endure hunger and thirst and wounds, and at the last your unwavering lines disap-pear into the smoke and wrath of battle. Bravest of the brave, most generous of the generous, never had country more faithful friends than you.

These words could have been written by Bill, who lived and fought alongside the Gurkhas and shared the darkest of days and nights. Bill never ate before his men had their food, a tradition he upheld within our family.

Bill and I visited Nepal, the Gurkha homeland, in 1978 on our Bales tour. A little like the houses in Zanskar, the dwellings were well made, with steeply sloping roofs and fine wooden carving. The ground floor was for the animals. We went to Badgaon near Kathmandu and walked round a huge square where earthenware pots of all shapes and sizes were being made or lying in the sun to dry. An old man was playing a little stringed instrument, a *saringi*. It was enchanting.

Next we moved onto to the Pashupatinath Temple on the Bagmati river which is to the Nepalis what the Ganges is to the Indians. It is believed to be sacred and a most blessed place in which to die. The old and the ill are brought here as they near their life's end and are cared for in a simple way by relatives or friends. The shining white temple stands in a square in the middle of a bridge which spans the river. It is surrounded by holy men, by jewellery vendors, fruit sellers, merchants displaying the brilliant powders – red, blue, yellow and orange – used for facial decoration like the 'tika' mark on the forehead.

Below, in the slow-moving murky water people bathed, washed clothes and cooking pots. Here, too, cremations were performed – though not while we were there. And there were beggars, some of the most tragic I have ever seen. Mutilated at birth means the child would always have a 'trade', begging. They heaved their poor bodies up steps and across stony ground to stretch out for the few coins that might drop into their hands. Such wretched lives on this earth surely must find these unfortunate victims a better place in the after-life. A band played. Life and death were cheek by jowl. It was moving, poignant, and I couldn't concentrate on our visit to the largest *stupa* (Buddhist Temple) in the world. It was enormous, and awash with fluttering prayer flags which reached up to the dome. Hundreds of prayer wheels surrounded it, waiting for the hands to set them spinning clockwise and the prayers spinning upwards.

Here life took precedence over death: shops, dwellings inhabited by monks, mothers breast-feeding, women sweeping grain onto mats; but somehow here the atmosphere was much more muted than at Pashupatinath. Perhaps there, although death was still present, there was a sense of blessed release from a life of hardship or pain, and a kind of calm joy at the spirit being freed into another existence.

Less enchanting was our arrival at the border with China. We saw, on the hill before us, the guard post. We had travelled north through increasingly infertile country. The rocky road was being repaired by both men and women who, like a chain-gang of white-dust ghosts, were heaving huge stones and then breaking them into smaller pieces. The last village before the border was the home of the Sherpas. Handsome people, more basic dwellings, warmer, thicker clothes. And then the simple bridge, the connection between Nepal and Tibet, guarded at each end. The bridge which seemed to divide two worlds instead of connecting them. The sun blazed off the huge binoculars that were trained on us as we stood on the other side of the 'no go' area. The vibrant, bustling, warm energy of the Nepali villages and people had vanished. We stood in silence.

We drove back, thinking our own thoughts, and waited quietly while the driver fixed a problem in the engine. The sun disappeared as we broke down yet again. The driver hopped out once more and piled rocks inside the engine. Our tour leader asked him why. It was to keep everything firm. 'Oh yes, of course', she said, 'I see.' Wonderful British cool!

Nepal, Burma, Tibet – why is it that these extraordinary countries, with their beautiful people and fascinating cultures, are so vulnerable? Why can't they be left alone?

THE FAR East holds a deep fascination for me. Alas, the nearest I got to Malaya, as it was called in the 1950s, was in Pinewood Studios, filming *A Town Like Alice*. There was second unit filming in Malaya itself, long shots of the exhausted, bedraggled women and children struggling through the jungle, from camp to camp: you really couldn't tell that none of us actors ever left England! The back projection scenes were so well done, no-one recognised that the sweat on our brows as we waded through the 'swamps' of Burnham Beeches, not far from Pinewood, was really drops of glycerine. Far from being hot and steamy, it was extremely chilly and blankets and a warm toddy awaited us when we damply emerged from the water. It looked real, but it also felt real.

It was a major cast, headed by the handsome, charismatic Peter Finch. His 'mate' was Vincent Ball, fondly known as Snowy, who is

Top: With Peter Finch in A Town Like Alice.

Left: With Jack Lee, the director.

Bottom: The women POWs wade through the 'swamps' of Burnham Beeches!

still a friend. The film was based on a true story, and on the book written by Nevil Shute. The actresses who made up our little band of weary travellers were all wonderful and greatly respected. My beloved Marie Lohr, Renée Houston, Jean Anderson, Nora Nicholson, Eileen Moore, Maureen Swanson, to name a few. The diminutive Japanese soldier in charge of us all, whom we 'prisoners' all grew fond of, was actually a lampshade maker from Shepherd's Bush.

The people who created and built the sets at Pinewood were masterful. The office where we worked and received the news of the Japanese invasion; the house where women and children rested on the journey; the compound where we plucked chickens (that Joe, Peter Finch, had stolen for us to eat); the huge tree in the forest where Joe was 'crucified'; the Malayan village where, at last, the much-reduced band of bedraggled women and children found a haven, all were intensely real. As we became more tired, our clothes more tattered, our hair more dishevelled, the more we seemed to be able to reach the heart of the story. To such an extent that when my character, Jean Paget, all neat and tidy, had one scene in a lawyer's office and a final one at the 'airport' when she was reunited with Joe, I found it quite hard to keep it as true as the rest.

And then there were the children. It was the first time I had worked closely with children, and the start of a very special enjoyment and fascination. We grown-up actors struggle to convey a thought, a feeling, but a child just does it with a look. Our director Jack Lee, author Laurie Lee's brother, was an energetic, lively person and always supportive and enthusiastic. I met him again in the 1990s in Alice Springs (where I had never been before) at a charity showing of the film. My daughter Louise came with me, Snowy came with Jack and it rekindled our old friendships.

Jack died in Sydney in 2002, but there was a service in his childhood village of Slad in Gloucestershire, and a memorial ceremony was held afterwards on the hill above. The lush, fruit-laden, flower-scented, hay-warm, flood-filled, *Cider with Rosie* childhood days of the Lee family in 1918 filled my imagination as I looked down on the little houses. I felt a poignant nostalgia for those innocent times, filled though they were with the everyday challenges of life.

A Taste of Hollywood

LOS ANGELES. SUNSET BOULEVARD. Before Bill and I were married he was invited to Hollywood to appear in a remake of *The Painted Veil* by Somerset Maugham, playing opposite Eleanor Parker and co-starring George Sanders. As we weren't married we were not allowed to share an apartment. We were installed in two suites in the Beverly Wilshire Hotel. Bill was out working every day and, never one for a luxury lifestyle, I spent my time reading, tennis lessons and swimming. It all got a bit much and I asked Bill if he would like me to find an apartment: at least I could go food shopping and cook and look after the place. After scouring advertisements for several days, I came across an apartment with a large open terrace, on Sunset Boulevard, with an avocado tree within touching distance. It was just right in every way. The studio wasn't overly enthusiastic, but went along with the idea, providing they actually rented *two* apartments! I'm sure they knew we'd never use the second one but, as it turned out, it was providential.

On Sunset, you never knew which famous name would be up in lights outside the clubs and bars. Billie Holliday. Bill was a total fan of her musical style, her voice, and moved by the story of her difficult and tragic life, so when we saw her name illuminated above the door of a nightclub we wasted no time. We sat at a table and excitedly anticipated the moment when she would walk onto the little stage. Suddenly, we saw a lone figure sitting at the bar. 'That's Terence Rattigan,' we whispered. We didn't know him but felt he might like to join us, to share Billie's magic with us. He was quiet and charming and I always recalled this meeting when I played Hester in a television production of his play *The Deep Blue Sea*, with Peter Egan playing Freddie.

Billie's performance surpassed our expectations. Many songs later she left the stage, the lights dimmed, we said goodnight to Rattigan and went our separate ways. As we came outside we saw the 'other' Billie. Alone, walking a little dog along the pavement. No showbiz crowd, just a lady who carried on working to pay the bills. We felt quite sad.

Sunset Boulevard: on our terrace with Leslie Phillips.

Life for us was happy and fun and occasionally I would go to the studio and join Bill for lunch. That was really exciting. Kay Kendall was there, about to start filming *Les Girls* for George Cukor. She was sitting nearby and I heard her talking about a part that still hadn't been cast. She saw me and asked if I knew that blond, very English actor who was good at comedy.

'Leslie Phillips. He would be wonderful and he's a friend of ours.'

We had, not long before, worked with Leslie in the comedy *The Smallest Show on Earth* with Peter Sellers, Margaret Rutherford and Bernard Miles. Kay suggested Leslie, he was cast in the part, and he flew out to the West Coast and was ensconced in an hotel. But not for long! He was soon a happy occupant of our second apartment and joined us, on many an evening, for supper on our terrace.

The Painted Veil had been renamed *The Seventh Sin*. The production, for various reasons, had its ups and downs and, at one point, Bill found that he had three or four days off. By a stroke of luck Leslie was free too. So we jumped in the car and went off and had an adventure. We drove to Las Vegas. Across the Mojave Desert.

Even in 1956 Las Vegas was extraordinary. A foreign land: bars, casinos, nightclubs, Western saloons, vast hotels lined the streets. It was fantasy time. We decided, of all things, to go to see a striptease. Lili St Cyr was famous for her artistic and beautiful show. To reach the audience area, you had to pass through a casino lined with 'fruit machines' and gambling tables, all strangely calm. The fruit machine players were mainly middle-aged or older women. Their concentration was total as they put in the coins and cranked the handles. There were few shouts of triumph as we passed through and entered the more colourful, alive environment of the theatre.

Lili St Cyr truly was an artiste of the highest quality, and very beautiful. Her striptease (she was Carmen to an invisible Don Juan - a part assumed, I'm sure, by many of the men in the audience!) was sensuous but discreet.

After the show we 'hit' a saloon bar full of Stetson-wearing, beer-drinking cowboy types. It looked quite fun, so in we went. There were the usual fruit machines and Bill and Leslie decided to have a go. Suddenly, the person in charge of the gambling called out 'Next winner we'll pay double!' Bill and Leslie worked out some scheme whereby one would put the money in and the other pull the handle. I wandered off to have a look round when suddenly I heard a very English voice call out:

'I say, I say, we've done it!'

Total silence: all the faces turned to look at this extraordinary person with the most extraordinary accent! However, they had won, and it was smiles and back-slapping all round. We got to bed about 4 am.

The next day, we drove slowly to Los Angeles, enjoying the desert landscape with its cacti and rocks and wide skies. Bill found Hollywood a place of great insecurities. How you were greeted when you turned up for work depended on how good you had been in the 'rushes' - the material filmed the previous day and then watched and judged. If it was a short 'hello' and no arm round the shoulder you knew there was a problem. It was a strange few weeks; we met some delightful people, but we were, if I'm honest, happy to be going home to our little flat at the top of a friend's house in Chelsea. No avocados to reach out for, but we still had trees outside our windows.

Reflections, Lake Geneva

I N THE MID-1980S, BILL and I met Prince and Princess Sadruddin Aga Khan. He was uncle of the Aga Khan. We were invited to stay in their beautiful home on the shores of Lake Geneva. 'Sadri' was passionate about many things: refugees, injustice, the environment and animals. Passions shared by Princess Catherine (Katy). Katy was also active in several campaigns, particularly against wearing fur. She now funds a sanctuary for donkeys in Patmos. The house is filled with exquisite treasures and books reflecting ancient Muslim art and culture. One could have an amazing house, yet nothing more. But this house lives and breathes something you cannot find in an art gallery or library. It is the generosity of spirit of the two people whose home it is that fills each room and walks, tangibly, in the garden.

Sadri's spirit is everywhere. He died after a long and painful illness in 2003. The most modest, reasonable, quietly-spoken of men, he fought fiercely against intolerance and cruelty and for the preservation of his beloved Alps. We worked closely with his Bellerive Foundation in 1989, on the Elefriends campaign to save the elephants when my eldest son Will drove out from England, carrying 600,000 signatures against the ivory trade. Sadri presented the petition to the Chair of the CITES (Convention on International Trade in Endangered Species) Standing Committee. Together we mounted a significant display against this terrible and senseless commercial practice. On that occasion the campaign succeeded, and African elephants were put on Appendix I, totally protected by law against all trade.

Who could have imagined that nineteen years later the same gorgon would raise its head once more? In Kenya alone, 57 dead elephants have been found during the first eight months of 2008. This is fifteen per cent more than in the whole of 2007. More than half of these animals were found in the North, where teams of Chinese workers have moved in to tarmac miles and miles of gravel roadways. Is this a coincidence? We do know that the majority of people caught smuggling ivory out of the airport in Nairobi are Chinese. We do know that a great number of the tusks are hidden in trucks and carried over the

Prince and Princess Sadruddin Aga Khan (Sadri and Katy).

border into Ethiopia. Here it is cheaper to buy ivory in the markets than in mainland China. The temptation must be great, if you are determined to buy animals' teeth carved into trinkets.

The CITES decision-makers have a lot to answer for. How could they fail to understand that by now allowing China, as well as Japan, to buy 108,000 tonnes of ivory they have opened the cruel floodgates to death, suffering and fear. Don't they care that elephant families will be hunted down, torn apart, that bodies will lie mutilated on African soil, shocking evidence of man's greed and callousness. I suppose that when money is the god nothing is sacred.

It goes without saying that orphans will arrive at Daphne Sheldrick's elephant sanctuary outside Nairobi, but they will be the lucky ones. Sadri would be heartbroken.

⌣

THE HUGE trees that border the path create dappled patterns that subtly move beneath my feet. Boats, mirrored on the water, are all that disturb the calm surface of Lake Geneva. Here and there ducks paddle lazily by. A butterfly flutters beneath the trees.

As I write, I am back in that tiny paradise by Lake Geneva, for a few days with Katy, sharing memories, our concerns for the future of our trembling little earth and hoping, against all the odds, that the suffering of innocent humans and animals will one day be ended. The hope is, perhaps, forlorn, but we hang on to it all the same.

Those moments of silence and reflection that you can find in that beautiful home are, for me, gifts beyond price. Some people need to cram each minute with action, keeping busy, 'filling the day'. For me, the opposite is true. But I have a choice. How different it is for captive animals.

Inside the palm, beneath the searching fingers
The skin is pink and wrinkled
Just like mine.

Eyes beyond the mesh behind the glass
Look into my eyes
Same thoughts. I know.

Sad, mad monkey
In that twilight box.
Reflected in the glass,
Dim outline in that silent, sordid world.
I see myself, and you beyond.
Trapped. Forever.
In my memory.

What is your question?
Why?
Mine is the same.

The crazy, somersaulting mangabey in the Jardin des Plantes; the withdrawn panda in Beijing Zoo, or the frenetic one in the Shanghai Zoo; the caged polar bear in Shirotori Zoo in Japan, in a dark den with no water; the terrified bear, beaten as it desperately tried to overcome its fear as it was forced to walk a tightrope in the Shanghai Zoo; my memory photo album has new pages each day. And the old ones never fade.

Amongst the latest are images of goats and chickens and cows. Not wild animals, but animals fed, live, to awaiting lions or tigers, in an enclosure below, or surrounding the food wagon. A live chicken, dangled on a pole just out of reach of the predators' jaws, taunting and teasing them and finally torn from the pole by the frantic mouth. The cow, pushed out of the back of the truck into the enclosure where several big cats circle and wait. Not a quick death as with Girl and the gazelle. Here the cats were uncertain what to do. So many agonising minutes of fear were endured by the victim before the final *coup de grâce*.

'Why can't you do something?' I hear you scream. You are right. And as I write I am awaiting a response to a second letter I have written to a senior Chinese official in London. Just before the terrifying earthquake in China I had lunch in London, together with one of Born Free's Trustees, with three officials from the Embassy. I presented a dossier of the evidence and was politely assured this would be looked into. Then the earthquake. Then the Olympics. I waited out of respect for all these upheavals to pass. Then my two letters. Who knows if anything will happen, but I have received a response to my communications and I am hoping once more. I suppose what makes it all so much worse is that when the Chinese zoo visitors watch these 'spectacles', they laugh. They laugh. We weep.

What is freedom? Is 'Nature' ever free from us? Not if you read Matthew Parris' fascinating Opinion piece in *The Times* last summer (30 August 2008). And it is true. We control what bits of nature we will conserve, what bits we will allow to be invaded, what species we will protect and rescue (and, oh, yes, let's bring them into captivity to 'save' them). More frozen arks will mushroom around the world, and 'ooh' and 'aah' we will marvel as we gaze at these wonderful creatures in their so-called 'naturalistic' enclosures. Meanwhile, their real and ancient homes will have been over-run by palm oil plantantions, ever-burgeoning human activity or changed forever by the irreversible tread of climate change.

Have we forgotten that the complexity of nature is what makes our world fit to live in? Out of sight and, therefore, to us out of mind are the trillions of creatures and plants that have evolved over millions of years, species we carelessly hunt down, chop up, dig up, pollute, plunder from the oceans, throw away, like there is no tomorrow! And, if we don't listen to all the alarm bells now jangling, that is exactly what there will be. For us humans at least.

Doomed Elephants

BOUT FOUR YEARS AGO Will and I went to America. Our main aim was to visit the famous San Diego Zoo and Wild Animal Park. Bill and I had been there before and, contrary to all we had heard, we were fairly unimpressed with some of the 'exhibits'. On this occasion, Will and I went to see seven elephants 'rescued' from Swaziland. Four others had gone to Lowry Park Zoo in Florida. At that time, there were thirty-six elephants in Swaziland, living wild in two national Reserves. (It was said that the country was unable to sustain its elephant population.) Arguing that their removal would be detrimental to their well-being, Adam Roberts of Born Free USA (BFUSA) and others launched a lawsuit against the USA zoos. It nearly succeeded. It was only when the US judge was confronted with a message, from Swaziland, saying that refridgerator space had been reserved for the elephants' bodies that the exportation went ahead. That was 2003. Money played a big part in all this (about US$ 132,000 in fact). The rustle of paper or glint of gold is irresistible to some people. How many animals have been victims of trade and deals?

We went first to the Asian elephant enclosure with Adam and Florence Lambert, an American friend, passionate also about captive elephant issues. Here, a keeper dressed in safari gear, was talking to the audience whilst getting an elephant to lift its trunk, pick up a log and put its foot on a tub. In an adjoining area another elephant stood behind a barred gate, swaying endlessly from side to side. As a conservation message it was a farce. Sickened by what we heard and saw, we visited the Swaziland elephants, kept in the African ele enclosure up on the hill behind us. (The bull was isolated in a smaller pen.) One of the females had been pregnant and her calf was there with her, standing beside an empty wallow. The keeper explained there was no water in it as they were afraid the baby would drown! Will and I were speechless. 'Rescue.' For what? Life on a postage stamp in California a million miles away from home? All these magnificent, intelligent animals doomed never to move over the plains, select the grasses and browse, communicate with other elephant groups, be part of a whole wild landscape. Shades of Pole Pole came back to haunt me.

Above: April 4th 2000 – Will and I on College Green outside the House of Commons, for the BFF's 'Stop the Clock' campaign against poaching to supply the illegal trade in ivory.

Below: A bull elephant in Amboseli.

Two of the world's leading experts on elephants made their views plain. Daphne (Dr) Sheldrick, our friend from Pole Pole days, wrote:

> I cannot see how keeping elephants under the unnatural conditions of captivity can possibly contribute towards the 'conservation of the species' or be of any educational value. There is nothing educational in seeing a miserable captive, especially in this day when television can bring into every American home elephants enjoying a quality of life in wild terms.

Dr Cynthia Moss, who has famously headed the Amboseli Elephant Research Project in Kenya (part-funded since 1990 by Born Free), summed up the views of her colleagues and herself:

> In the case of elephants, with their potentially long lives, their ability to communicate their emotional states with numerous vocalisations and displays, their loyalty and care of each other, their gentleness and dignity, we believe the time has come to consider them as sentient beings and not as so much money on the hoof to be captured and sold and displayed for our own use. We should be beyond the exploitation of animals as complex and magnificent as elephants.

The elephants are blue
Blue in the evening's indigo
The dawn's first azure light

The elephants are red
Red from the terracotta soil's
Warm wallowed mantle

The elephants are silver
Moon ghosts between the trees
And shining through night's veil

The elephants are grey
Without disguise of light or night
Grey shadows in the forest

The elephants are gone
Mourned spirits in the air
Haunting our dreams.

〜

YES, I know, I have written a lot about elephants. But those little Swaziland lives changed for the worst, for the worst of reasons, by callous, self-interested, misguided people, became a symbol of all that is wrong about zoos. True, they are killed in the wild, but is a short natural life not better than a longer unnatural, hopeless one? And why does it have to be one or the other?

Fighting for Lives

CALCUTTA 1978. I STILL reel at the memory of our brief visit. What had I expected? Crowds? Squalor? It was all there, but when you actually see it, it is a thousand times more compelling than in a photograph or a film. People surging, milling, jostling, existing. At that time there were 20,000 people for each square kilometre. One and a half million Bangladeshi refugees scratched a desolate existence in the chaos of shacks and lean-tos which made up the refugee camp. A sea of grey rags, dirt. The bottom of society and with no hope of change. Here and there huge mounds of rubbish seemed to move as women and children climbed over them, seeking anything that could be eaten. Anything that could be used. Here the human engine abounds; the rickshaw man with his thin, pathetic body, his swollen knee joints, his bare feet (bare feet brake better), his tragic fare of half a rupee for a fifteen minute journey. One rupee, today, is worth about 7p. This was the Bangladeshi refugee camp, we were told. Home to hundreds. Home to people who had lost everything, including members of their own family.

We passed many of the 150,000 people who slept on the streets. Some on mats, some on rags, some on the bare dirty pavement, some on top of the public lavatory. Lying, sitting, staring. And then, in this extraordinary mosaic which is India, we found ourselves near the Victoria Memorial, surrounded by a shouting, flag-waving crowd. Bus and lorry-loads of people lurched by, people clinging to every handle and fender.

'You see,' our guide said, 'they are going to listen to Madam Gandhi who is speaking in the *Maidan* [a big park]. Only a month ago they were denouncing her, now they are for her. They want change in India - there is a strong political feeling.'

Our guide was brilliant. A sort of poetic realist, full of passion and imagery. The fiery globe of the sun setting over the river, the multitudes of people, even the poverty seemed to inspire him and set his eyes alight.

Virginia McKenna

Across an ocean of heads we saw, far away, the tiny, white sari-clad figure of Mrs Gandhi standing on a flag-decorated dais. How exhilarating it must be to arouse such extremes of passion.

'We are very emotional in Calcutta,' our guide said proudly. 'Oh yes, we are a city of demonstrations – you see, over there, is a communist demonstration. But it is a small candlestick in front of the sun.'

He told us that two women draw the crowds in India. Queen Victoria, who never visited the country but, in whose memory garlands of flowers are laid at the base of her statue at the Victoria Memorial. And Mrs Gandhi. To be tragically murdered in 1984.

'Calcutta is the city of life,' our guide said, 'the city of people. You can forget the buildings and the stones, but you cannot forget the people.'

He was right. I never have. After all these years.

⌣

NOW WE know the refugee camps are all over the world. However flimsy the shelters, they are home to hundreds of thousands, dependent on others for their survival and their safety. Vulnerable to every migrating disease or tribal conflict but, still, attempting to keep the few square feet they exist in clean and decent.

Celebrities use their fame to stand up for them and try to help, endeavouring to bypass politics and reach out to all people. Bob Geldof, Sting, Mia Farrow (my entrancing Peter Pan), Roger Moore, Bono, George Clooney, Joanna Lumley, the late Audrey Hepburn and many others have done more than just lend a name. They have gone out there, looked, become voices for the voiceless, been deeply humbled. They may sometimes feel helpless, powerless against the heavyweights of government and politics and tribal aggression, but it is easy to be disheartened, and of course they never are. They fight on.

The sea of rags in Calcutta, the ocean of tents in Darfur, the polar bear balancing on his pinhead of ice. This is the world we are all a part of. In the Arctic the ships are already penetrating waters hitherto inaccessible because of the ice. The ice landscape is melting. The polar bears' way of life is changing, inexorably.

I was once told that for a polar bear life in captivity is hell. A polar bear, unlike most other animals, does not have a territory: the world it inhabits is constantly changing with the seasons. So, what do the zoo people do? They impose a territory, usually a wretched one at that. Just having rocks and water isn't enough, as I saw when I visited Central Park Zoo in New York. One of the polar bears was swimming backwards and forwards, rising and twisting, plunging and turning, in exactly the same pattern for over half an hour.

So, if the ice floes melt, will the polar bears take Sarah Palin's advice and learn to live on land? That, of course, depends on whether there is any land to live on after the invasion of the oil wells.

Now at last, is some good news to supply the much-needed balance. To warm our hearts, give us hope. The Gurkhas' case in the High Court has been won! The brave, selfless men who fought for Britain, who risked their lives for us, are going to be allowed to live here. This battle has been won without guns. Now the government must accept the Court's decision. It must speak out.

However, many weeks on it is still 'considering'. I joined a very large gathering in Parliament Square in late November with Joanna, Peter Carroll, cross-party MPs and Gurkha veterans. A message was read out from Boris Johnson, London's Mayor; Glenda Jackson MP arrived to give her support. The Square was filled with Britons, Gurkhas, all in a state of disbelief that our leaders were still prevaricating over the 1997 cut-off date. This date, seemingly plucked out of the air, dictating the fate of a relatively small number of men who had risked all for this country. My personal joy today was that I was able to shake the hand of the 91-year-old veteran, Lachhiman Gurung VC.

A hundred of us were allowed to walk to the Cenotaph to lay a wreath in memory of those who died. Then (as in the Burma demo outside the Chinese Embassy), we were herded into a wire-meshed area on the far side of the road from Downing Street. Eventually, six Gurkha representatives, with Joanna, would be allowed into Downing Street carrying the bags containing nearly a quarter of a million signatures.

In my mind there is no doubt that Joanna's unflinching dedication to their cause played an enormous part in the public's support of this campaign. The news coverage was in depth and serious, the campaign excellently co-ordinated by Peter Carroll, and the cause itself stirred feelings of outrage and astonishment in all of us who believe in justice and decency.

Moscow Interlude

RED SQUARE IS ENORMOUS. And so was the queue of people slowly snaking its way across to the mausoleum to visit Lenin and Stalin in their glass cases. A small step out of line and a uniformed soldier would march up and sternly put you back in your place. Like a school crocodile we dutifully shuffled to see two of the most famous men who had ever lived. Loved and admired by some. Loathed by others.

We were invited by the State to the Moscow Film Festival. *Two Living One Dead* was being shown, a film Bill and I made in 1960, based on the book by the Norwegian prize-winning author Sigurd Christiansen. Back in 1960 it had been directed by the brilliant Anthony Asquith ('Puffin') and starred Patrick McGoohan. We had filmed it in Sweden in late autumn, so the daylight was brief and the nights long.

Apart from the joy of having our little children Will and Louise with us, two things stick out in my mind: all of us playing fiercely competitive games of Racing Demon with Puffin in the evenings; and Bill and I getting oyster poisoning. One of the 'starters' at dinner was three oysters. Not a connoisseur of oysters, I wasn't sure if they tasted right or not. After eating two I offered the third to Bill. Unfortunately he accepted it! We have never been so ill. We phoned for the doctor at about 1 am. He gave us injections to stop the sickness and we collapsed on the bed until the alarm rang to get us up for work. By lucky chance the scene was a funeral and my hat had a nice thick veil, hiding my ashen face. In fact the embalmed faces of Lenin and Stalin were healthier-looking than mine!

As we reached the steps leading down into the chamber all talking was forbidden. In silence we descended into the increasingly cool atmosphere. And there they were. In uniform, adorned with medals and with hands neatly folded on their chests: a strange experience. I heard not long afterwards that Stalin had been 'demoted', and his remains interred within the Kremlin wall alongside other well-known figures in Soviet history.

The mausoleum may have been cool but the Russian people we met were warm and welcoming. We had a few events to attend, but apart from that we were taken on a river trip, walked on our own around the streets and went to some lively parties. It was rather humbling too. The Russians knew a lot about our English writers and playwrights but we knew comparatively little about theirs!

One evening a most touching thing happened. The group of actors and actresses we had made friends with turned up at a delightful dinner on our last night. Suddenly one of them, Lydia, got up, took off her lovely necklace and put it round my neck. Her husband, Oleg, gave Bill his tie. Such spontaneous generosity from people who had few luxuries in their lives. We kept in touch with them for several years.

We had travelled out on a Russian plane (plans were suddenly changed at the last minute but no-one explained why). It turned out that Yuri Gagarin, the first man in space, was on the same flight! I got his autograph. Another travelling companion was a nephew of Stanislavski. We got talking and he asked if we would like to go with him to his uncle's house in Moscow. We couldn't wait! This was a highlight of our trip. He collected us at the 'Moskva' hotel (large and soulless) and, excited, we went with him.

The door was opened by an elderly lady, the housekeeper, who welcomed our friend effusively. After a few minutes' greeting, we wandered slowly round the house, filled with poignant reminders of his life, to absorb it all. His study had been left as it was, his desk, his books. One visitor to the house when Stanislavski was alive had written:

> It was with a feeling of deep emotion and joy that we entered Stanislavski's house: a tall old man with snow white hair rose from the arm chair to greet us. It was enough for us to converse with Stanislavski just five to ten minutes to come away feeling like a new born person, cleansed of all that might be 'bad' in art.

This extraordinary man who was blessed with genius, opened the world of theatre and acting to a completely new approach. Years ago people joked about 'method' acting – how one had to sit and try to 'be' a teapot or a tree. But, of course, it wasn't about that at all. It was about actors trying to express truthful feelings in whatever circumstances their characters found themselves.

We protested against the old manner of acting, Stanislavski wrote, and against theatricality, against artificial pathos and declamation, and against affectation on the stage, and inferior conventional productions and decoration, against the star system which had been a bad effect on the cast...

Stanislavski believed that 'to seek those roads into the secret sources of inspiration must serve as the fundamental life problem of every true actor'.

There are still many great actors today who follow this concept. But there are many others who, under pressure to deliver 'instant results', or who have the right 'look', with insufficient time in rehearsal, cannot delve into the 'secret sources of inspiration' and have no option but to skim the surface. We live in an instant world.

More Zoo Checks

I T IS EARLY DAWN. The dew gleams. Few creatures stir except ourselves. We are a small group of travellers on safari in India, and about to set off on a coracle ride on the Kabini river. Coracles are amazing, half-a-walnut-shell shaped crafts. They are usually made from a framework of willow; in former times this was covered with animal skin but now this has been replaced by calico or canvas. The beauty of it is that it is silent. No engine, just a man and a paddle. As we set forth, we could see a few spiky branches of dead trees poking through the mist, but nothing more. It was a hidden world which only gradually revealed itself as the sun burned through. Then – little islands, storks, egrets, herons, ducks – the world began to awaken.

Later we took a boat down the river and saw elephants on the bank, drinking, splashing about. On the opposite side, small groups of women filled their water pitchers, gossiped and waved. Remembering it now I have a longing to go back, to stay at the Kabini River Lodge managed by Colonel John Wakefield. He had been so generous to us with his time, telling us stories of India 'in the old days'. Certainly his tiny patch retained its charm and tranquillity. We sat round the open fire in the evening and watched local people perform the 'stick dance' for us. Followed by delicious curries – of course!

This wasn't the end of our magical journey. The next stop was Mysore, to the white Lalitha Mahal Palace Hotel, the magnificent City Palace, where we discovered that many of the materials – iron and glass – had been brought from England and Glasgow! We visited the market with its dazzling, brightly-coloured mounds of spices and powders, flowers, vegetables and fruit – aromas to make you swoon! Out in the street vehicles and bicycles jostled and shared the space with cows and children and street vendors, tiny tailor shops with whirring sewing machines, barrows selling freshly-made chapattis and samosas.

Of course, I went to the zoo. Here and there attempts had been made to 'enrich' the spaces but, inevitably, a zoo is a zoo. Two elephants were tethered; a white tiger paced its concrete indoor cage frustratedly. From the row of carnivore cages emerged occasional roars. Each of

Virginia McKenna

Above: Our coracle ride on the Kabini river.

Right: Flying foxes, herons and egrets in the Ranganathittu Bird Sanctuary.

Below: The mounds of highly-coloured spices and powders in the market in Mysore.

the animals would have to take it in turn to go into the single outside area. I estimated once a week – if they were lucky. It is difficult to go into a zoo or leave it with any sense of cheerfulness, and that is something I deal with in my own way. I know I can't help all the animals I see but at least I can tell people about them. They are not forgotten.

The Ranganathittu Bird Sanctuary lifted my spirits. I love to relive our quiet, incredible watery journey over the lake which mirrored the forests of figs, bamboo, eucalyptus and acacia which border the banks. These spectacular trees are home to hordes of flying foxes – some of which hung like black, half-closed umbrellas, others which swooped between the branches. Dotted all over the sanctuary water are little islands, each with their different vegetation and home to nesting open-billed storks, spoonbills (always one of my favourites), painted storks, egrets and herons. Smaller birds nest in holes in the steep banks of the islands. We were lucky to see the iridescent flash of kingfishers and the deceptively immobile shapes of marsh crocodiles sunbathing on the rocks. We were lucky in every way. And so were the tigers that we transported back to India in 2002.

Rather like those we rescued in 1986, the five tigers from an Italian circus, Circo de Madrid, were only saved because the owner didn't have the paperwork for them! They too had lived in a circus trailer, deprived of exercise, in this case for at least eighteen months (apart from performing in the ring).

There is always something awesome about tigers. Zeudy, Harak and King were no exception, nor were their companions Taras and Royale. They first went to the Kent Sanctuary in 1997, where the larger space encouraged them to be very territorial, very challenging. We hastily built another enclosure. But, as so sadly happens, not all animals can overcome their past lack of care and Taras died just over a year later of liver failure and cancer of the spleen – only a few months before we were to move all the tigers to a second sanctuary we had made in Karnataka in India.

Another tiger, little Roque, was for sale in a pet shop in Barcelona. We investigated under cover and, eventually, after a few months at a halfway house in Spain while the paperwork was completed, he too came to Kent. He was five months old. We gathered he had been taken away from his mother only three days after he was born, sold by a Belgian dealer and eventually ended up in the shop. Thank God we took him away from that part of his life and were able to give him a

Virginia McKenna

Above: Roque the tiger in a Barcelona pet shop.
Below: Roque in the Bannerghatta Sanctuary in India.

happier future. Far removed from the trade scenario where animals are sold and bartered for as if they were bags of sugar. (Although some might call it maintaining a varied gene pool).

And then, of course, there was 'Ginny'. She and 'Bill' had been rescued from de Limburgse Zoo in Belgium in a project fronted by Jenny Seagrove. It was she who named these two tigers. Bill and I were very touched.

I shall never forget the extraordinary trip I made to de Limburgse in 1996, with a journalist and photographer. My first visit had been with Bill in 1989. He had been on one of his zoo-checking trips in Holland and Belgium and had come home incensed and horrified by much of what he had seen. Particularly at this zoo. He wanted me to see it too, so we took the car ferry.

On my second visit little had changed. The air of melancholy was as heavy as before. The abnormal behaviour of many of the animals, the over-crowding in the baboon cages, the dark indoor chimp cages – well, it was just heartbreaking. The owner of the zoo knew we were coming and allowed us to wander around for about three hours. As we watched a brown bear stumbling around in a narrow pit, he suddenly turned up in his car and told us to return to the main building. His house. He sat us down at a small table in a gloomy hall. I remember there were a few stuffed animals here. Then, suddenly, we were surrounded by other members of the family. Wife, grandmother, son – all vehemently shouting at us. Blaming the BBC and Zoo Check for the demise of the zoo. Upholding their belief that no animal should be euthanased, however much it was suffering. A press cutting of the Queen Mother was shoved under my nose as they shouted: 'She is 95 and you don't euthanase her!' I suggested it was hardly a convincing comparison. We were dragged into the indoor night quarters, which held several of the big cats – including a seriously lame male lion. The stench made us reel. The experience made us sick to our stomachs. The zoo mercifully did close.

Tiger Bill was wracked with acute pancreatitis, from which he never recovered. He was euthanased in April 1997. Ginny mourned – what a life sentence they had endured together at the zoo. What a different life they experienced together at the Sanctuary. All too briefly. But Ginny was on her way to India with the others. The vet, John Kenward, who was in charge of them, believed her more fragile disposition would not be a problem (and indeed it wasn't; she didn't need any sedative and was as calm as the rest!). Amanda Holden was a part of our team - as enthusiastic and supportive as she has always been. Our great disappointment was that Jenny wasn't free to come. It would have meant so much to her to see Ginny in her spiritual home.

In 2002 Zeudy, Harak, King, Royale, Ginny and Roque were exploring their new territories, soaking in their pools, breathing warm Indian air. The huge Royale, so magnificent and regal, sadly succumbed to kidney failure five years later. Ginny too has gone. But peacefully. After two years of contentment. The others thrive and Roque, a stunning ten year old, is as wild as it is possible to be in a sanctuary.

Wild animals in the wild also fall victim to man's machinations. Masti is a wild tiger. He had been caught in a trap set for wild boar in a forest, and so half of his left foreleg needed to be amputated. For two years he had been captive in a cage at the forestry centre, but when an enclosure at our Sanctuary became free after the death of our old tiger Greenwich, we brought him there. Masti is really wild! Very aggressive towards humans and protests strongly if anyone goes too close. But when he feels he is not being observed he spends hours soaking in his pool or lying under the trees. His pool is cooling, soothing. Perhaps his dip is the best moment of his day.

HOW DIFFERENT are the pools in which dolphins are kept in captivity. How agonisingly different from the vibrant, ever-moving and changing oceans, where they live in harmony with their environment. The dolphin, creature of myth and legend, a species that even has its own heavenly constellation of ten stars, friend to man. Left alone it would carry on in its own way - hunting and leaping and playing and interacting with each other until...

Nature, they say, has caused the dolphin to be in perpetual motion, and for the dolphin, motion ends with the end of life.
Aelian (Claudius Aelianus), 'On Animals XI'

But have you seen dolphins in an aquarium? 'Hanging', motionless, by the side of the concrete holding pool? Have you smelled the chlorine in the water of their barren prison? Have you been taken in by their 'smile'?

Right: Rocky the dolphin in captivity in Morecambe Dolphinarium.

Below: Rocky, Missie and Silver are released.

Bottom: The 'Into the Blue' Mail on Sunday appeal for the release of the last three captive dolphins in the UK, 1991. With Jackie Pallo, Rula Lenska, Jenny Seagrove and Clare Francis.

Virginia McKenna

Prince Sadruddin summed it up so succinctly at the Bellerive Symposium on Whales and Dolphins in Captivity in 1990.

> As the dolphin becomes just another victim of humanity's utilitarian attitudes towards the Earth, it seems as though the ancient friendship between our respective species is no longer entirely reciprocal... Stripped of their natural identity, deprived of their own culture and environment, the dolphin and whale incarcerated within the oceanarium not only symbolise an abuse of that ancient relationship, but above all our estrangement from nature as a whole.

There were three dolphinaria in England. One in Morecambe; another in Yorkshire (Flamingoland); the third in Brighton. The plight of the solitary Rocky in Morecambe in 1989 had distressed a caring young woman, Bev Cowley, who began a campaign to try and help this vulnerable animal. Existing within a stone's throw of the sounds and sight of the sea.

In Brighton another young woman, Lucy Maiden, began a similar struggle on behalf of Missie and Silver. I joined a march along the Brighton seafront as, gradually, public opinion strengthened. The mood was changing.

What sealed the decision to close both places was a new 'standards' law for dolphinaria. Larger, deeper pools would have to be built. The owners would have to dig deep into their pockets as well. Rocky's owner generously gave him to the project. Brighton was sold to Sea Life Centres.

In 1990 the 'Into the Blue' campaign was born, supported by actors, actresses, sportsmen, friends, the world and his wife. At least that was one side of the coin. When the coin was flipped an unforeseen and aggressive face appeared, members of the dolphin 'industry', concerned about the threat to their livelihood. Naively, we thought everyone would be pleased that these three beautiful animals, having been incarcerated for most of their lives, were now being given a chance to learn to be wild again. The gloves were off. They had spirited Rocky away from Morecambe to Flamingoland after he had been given to the project. So we went to court. Seven stressful weeks later, finally, Rocky was on his way. Missie and Silver, who had also been given to the project by their owners, eventually joined him in a natural lagoon sanctuary in Providenciales, in the Turks and Caicos

Islands. There they would spend several months, learning to feed on live fish, being carefully observed by the expert team, having health checks from Dr Richard Kock and his colleagues. And they would be in the sea! At last.

Just before the release Will and I flew out. Angus MacPherson from *The Mail on Sunday* (the paper that had supported us from the start) was with us on the boat which went out to the release site, twelve miles offshore. It had been a wild morning, fitting perhaps for a wild event. But all became calm and we watched as our three dolphins swam around in their ocean release pen. Within moments the gate was opened. Rocky went first, coming back a few times as if to reassure the others. Then they were gone. The pen was empty. Our hearts were full.

What made this even more special was that our team included two men who had previously been part of that captive dolphin world. Doug Cartlidge, who had been a trainer at Flamingoland, and Gordon Panitzke, who had actually been with the people who captured Missie in 1969. This day both were happy men.

Of course, you never know for sure if rehabilitation will really work. You do your best, try to anticipate what problems the animal will have to face and prepare it as efficiently you can. But for our dolphins the omens looked good. Over the following four months they were seen over 25 times, singly or together (identified by the 'freeze brand' marking on their dorsal fin). They were taking their chance in the wild, but don't you think a year of freedom is better than twenty in captivity?

Dolphin

Mona Lisa of oceans
Your sunshine smile beguiles
Enchants and gathers us
Into your silver-sprayed
Arc-en-ciel.

In ocean or pool your joy
Blinds us to your secrets.

Virginia McKenna

Your glistening beauty,
Your tolerance of us –
Who also hide behind a mask of mirth –
Pierce the hearts of some who watch
The chlorine-scented show,
Far from the dolphin's deep and distant home
Light years from its origins
In nature's amphitheatre.

They say the elephant weeps salt tears.
The dolphin, creature of salt expanses,
Conceals its pain.
Locked in its smile as hopelessly
As we have land-locked it,
In concrete worlds of artificial sea.

Confirming my feelings about leaving wild animals to be themselves, Ric O'Barry (who had trained Flipper the dolphin of TV fame and who was a part of 'Into the Blue') wrote: 'They do us no harm. They wish us none, and we should leave them alone'.

Will and I actually swam in the sea near a wild dolphin. Friendly JoJo frequented the coast of Providenciales and, although he didn't come up to everyone, he had a very close relationship with a young American called Dean, Warden of the local National Parks. Dean took us out in a boat to see if we could find JoJo. It was a beautiful day, sparkling crystal blue sea, blue skies and our hearts were light as we thought of our dolphins swimming free. JoJo came near the boat and all of us, including a big black dog called Shaka, jumped into the water and watched through our masks as JoJo and Dean swam and spiralled down to the ocean floor. Shaka's legs paddled away furiously and for fifteen minutes we were out of this world. Silence, wonder, beauty, magic.

This dolphin experience strengthened me to face up to criticism. Not the slings and arrows of outrageous fortune, but the insults directed at you by people who dislike who you are, what you do and what you stand for. As an actor one is particularly vulnerable. A performance may attract sharp, negative comments, sometimes difficult to handle as confidence plays a big part in an actor's toolkit. But, however biting the review, you still have to go on stage the next night and play your part! That can take some doing! Yet it is a good lesson for other aspects of life too. In my case, I have never minded being criticised by those whose opinions I respect. Then I'll look, listen and try to learn. But, in our animal work, one is always a target for negative comments, often quite vitriolic, and it is important to put things in perspective.

I just think, 'Well, perhaps we have rattled their cage'. Good. As long as wild animals are in captivity and nothing changes, our message will be the same. How can it be otherwise?

What is the Earth?

What is the earth?
A ball in space?
A little paradise?
Planet of melting ice
And inner fires?

Under my hand
Its surface crumbles
Crushed underfoot
Its myriad flowers.

Forests lie trembling
Under my sword
The ocean darkens
Weeping black tears.

Death of sweet rivers
Death-giving rain
Silent and secret
Invisible pain.

A gift from heaven
This little world
Each bird a jewel
Each tree a mother.

What is the earth?
A fragile heart.
Tender my touch
To save its life –
And mine.

Virginia McKenna

Epilogue

TIME ONCE more to lift the geraniums and plant the tubs with bulbs. We need those bright little faces to lighten February days. Now I'm going to the churchyard, to tidy two graves, trim the grass and leave some loving thoughts behind me when my work is done. These moments are precious to me, as treasured as time spent with my children and grandchildren at Christmas, as we sit round the old table with its candles and crackers.

Like many people I go to church at Christmas. Part of me is already in our Christian churchyard, and one day the rest of me will follow. But I am open to all religions: at the heart of each of them, I believe, there are messages of kindness, generosity, peace and forgiveness. I say my prayers to whatever spirit fills the skies, to whatever is beyond the material, visible world. We all follow different paths, and as long as the path brings no harm, causes no pain, we should all be free to tread it.

Index

Photograph Credits

Oberon Books would like to thank the following for their kind permission to reproduce the images in this book. Every effort has been made to trace and contact the photographers and copyright holders. (AC = author's collection; T = top; B = bottom; C = centre; L = left; R = right.)